Waterside ~~~~~~
in Kent

David & Hilary Staines

COUNTRYSIDE BOOKS
NEWBURY BERKSHIRE

COUNTRYSIDE BOOKS
3 Catherine Road
Newbury, Berkshire

To view our complete range of books please visit us at
www.countrysidebooks.co.uk

All photographs by David Staines

ISBN 978 1 84674 408 2

*All materials used in the manufacture of this book
carry FSC certification.*

Produced through The Letterworks Ltd., Reading
Designed and Typeset by KT Designs, St Helens
Printed by Holywell Press, Oxford

CONTENTS

INTRODUCTION

With coastline making up half of the county's border, it's not surprising that Kent is home to a superb selection of waterside walks. Add to that an eclectic mix of rivers, lakes and one of the few canals in this corner of England, and the Kentish walker is spoilt for choice when it comes to fascinating walks by the water. However, this book is about more than just walking. There are things to see and do along the way, beautiful landscapes to discover, and history and heritage to uncover – everything to help you make the most of the great outdoors.

Here we have chosen 20 circular routes showcasing the best that the Garden of England has to offer. You'll find walks in the countryside, of course, but there are also routes along clifftops, beaches and seafronts; through historic villages and towns; alongside wide-open marshes and even a harbour arm. These walks take you from tiny hamlets to the county's greatest city.

Places of interest are highlighted throughout, so hopefully you'll get a sense of Kent's rich and intriguing history.

Each of these walks has been specially surveyed for this book, but please note that changes to paths, gates and stiles are not infrequent. If in any doubt about either the progress or safety of the route, always be prepared to turn round and retrace your steps to the starting place. Don't risk harm to yourself or getting seriously lost.

We also advise you to take or download the relevant Ordnance Survey map – we always give details of the relevant sheet as part of the walk. The latest editions of the 1:25000 series are by far the best.

In order to assist in getting you to the starting point of the walk, we have included the nearest postcode, although of course a postcode cannot deliver you to a precise starting point, especially in rural areas. And if you do plan to leave your vehicle in a pub car park, it's also wise to first ask at the bar whether it's OK to do so.

Enjoy!

David & Hilary Staines

PUBLISHER'S NOTE

We hope that you obtain considerable enjoyment from this book; great care has been taken in its preparation. Although at the time of publication all routes followed public rights of way or permitted paths, diversion orders can be made and permissions withdrawn.

We cannot, of course, be held responsible for such diversion orders or any inaccuracies in the text which result from these or any other changes to the routes, nor any damage which might result from walkers trespassing on private property. We are anxious, though, that all the details covering the walks are kept up to date, and would therefore welcome information from readers which would be relevant to future editions.

The simple sketch maps that accompany the walks in this book are based on notes made by the author whilst surveying the routes on the ground. They are designed to show you how to reach the start and to point out the main features of the overall circuit, and they contain a progression of numbers that relate to the paragraphs of the text.

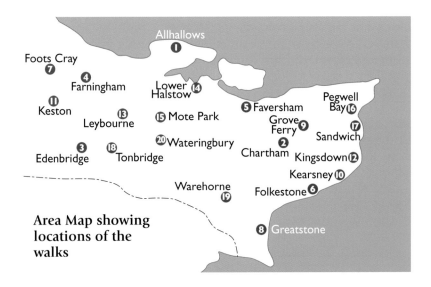

Area Map showing locations of the walks

Walk 1
ALLHALLOWS-ON-SEA
4 miles (6.4 km)

Start: Avery Way. **Sat Nav:** ME3 9QF.

Parking: Unrestricted parking in Avery Way near the village shop.

Map: OS Explorer 163, Gravesend & Rochester.
Grid Ref: TQ840783.

This walk, taking in the Thames Estuary and Yantlet Creek, is full of interest. Allhallows-on-Sea is the resort that never was. Look across the estuary and bustling Southend-on-Sea looms on the horizon. In the 1930s, Southern Railway hit on the idea that whatever Essex could do across the water, Kent would not just match, but vastly exceed. All it needed was a bit of stimulation. Why not buy some land in the middle of nowhere right opposite Southend, build a railway to it and sit back and wait for the inevitable visitors to arrive? The largest swimming pool in the UK was planned (complete with the first artificial wave generator in Europe) together with an amusement park four times the size of the one at Blackpool. Southern Railway duly built the railway, sat back and waited… and waited. The

---

> **Terrain:** No significant gradients, mostly flat sea wall and footpaths across the marshes.
>
> **Livestock & Stiles:** Cattle grazing on the marshes. One stile.
>
> **Dog Friendly?** Unfortunately the single stile on the walk does not have enough space for a large dog to pass through, and we cannot rule out the possibility that since our last visit even this gap may become obstructed.

reality of Allhallows-on-Sea didn't match the fantasy and nothing was ever built except a solitary Art Deco-style block of flats, a pub and a short length of promenade by the shoreline. All of which gives this place a unique appeal, providing an intriguing backdrop for a coastal stroll taking in marshland, sea walls and cracking views.

THE FENN BELL INN (unique in Kent with its own small zoo next door!) is a family-friendly pub on the Ratcliffe Highway near the A228 roundabout. ☎ 01634 270422. Limited supplies for an al-fresco picnic on the sea wall can be picked up from the village shop in Avery Way.

The Walk

1 From Avery Way head towards the holiday park, and then follow the sign-posted footpath into the holiday park to the left-hand side of the main entrance. Follow the drive past the gatehouse on the right and a further gatehouse on the left. Then take the next drive sign-posted Lake View, (this has been confirmed with the holiday village as the right of way). Follow the drive and track to the very bottom of the hill, you will see the sea at the bottom. When you get to the sea wall embankment, turn right keeping the sea on your left-hand side. At this point take a look behind you – this would have been the curving promenade of the resort; only the railings were ever built.

2 Now set off along the top of the sea wall keeping the sea on your left-hand side. This part of the walk is along the official Thames Path. Across the estuary Southend-on-Sea is on the horizon.

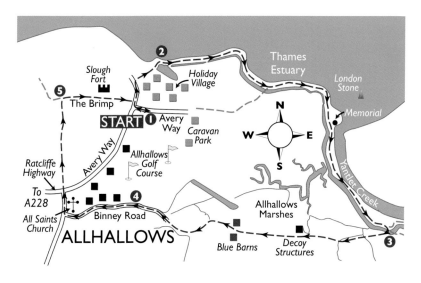

Follow the path on top of the sea wall keeping the sea on the left-hand side. After a while you turn into Yantlet creek. *Further out in the estuary, beyond the navigation marker you can just make out the "London Stone", an obelisk dating from 1856 which marks the point 34 miles from London Bridge where officially the Thames Estuary (and the jurisdiction of the Port of London Authority) ceases and the open sea begins.* Keep your eye on the watercourse on your right-hand side. After about ½ mile watch out for the first place you can cross this watercourse. At the same time the path you're on will turn sharply to the left.

❸ At this point turn right off the sea wall path and cross the watercourse. To start with the path here is almost invisible. Don't worry. With your back to the watercourse you need to bear right as if at 2 o'clock on a clock face. Don't be concerned if you can't see the path. Look for the blue barns and the radar tower on the low hillside in the distance and head in that direction - you will later be walking between those barns. A few metres later the path will become more apparent, keep the small watercourse on your right-hand side. In a very short while you will see a white metal gate at the end of the field line. This is the direction you're heading in. *Take a few minutes to look at the concrete structures on the right-hand side just before you reach the gate. What you see here are*

Slough Fort

the remains of a wartime decoy protecting a nearby oil refinery where rings of fuel would be set alight on the marshes to confuse the enemy bombers. The semi-circular structures were supports for the supplying fuel tank and the hapless servicemen encouraging the bombs to rain down on them would have to brave it out in the reinforced concrete shelter. Once over the stile next to the gate keep going through the field in the same direction. If at any stage on the marshes you are ever concerned about where you should be heading, keep heading in the direction of the two large blue barns. After you have passed them, follow the track as it twists and turns back towards Allhallows-on-Sea. *Along the way you will pass through a set of gates hung on concrete posts that are clearly much older. This was a crossing over the old railway line into Allhallows-on-Sea station, which lingered on until 1961, the trains disappearing with the dream of the resort. If you look to your right you can just make out the water tower used to provide water for the steam locomotives, still standing in the middle of the caravan park.*

4 When you come to the residential road, keep left along Binney Road to the far end. At the end of the road turn right passing All Saints Church on the corner. At the T-junction at the end of the next road, take the footpath across the field straight ahead.

5 When you get to the end of the field, with views of the sea again, turn right along the path. Soon Slough Fort will be on your left. *Slough Fort is a small D-shaped artillery fort built in 1867, overlooking and intended to guard a vulnerable stretch of the River Thames against possible landings by the French during a time of heightened concern about invasion. It is open to the public on the Sunday and Monday of Bank Holiday weekends and at other times for guided tours.* www.sloughfort.org.uk Continue to the end of the track, a quick right and sharp left will bring you back to the starting point at the post office and village shop.

Milton Riverside

Walk 2
CHARTHAM
2½, 4 or 8 miles (4, 6.4 or 12.8 km)

Start: The Green, Chartham. Sat Nav: CT4 7HX.

Parking: There is unrestricted parking in the village, park alongside the Green.

Map: OS Explorer 150 Canterbury & Isle of Thanet.
Grid Ref: TR105551.

This walk can be as short or ambitious as you want. Chartham, an archetypal English village with a church and a tranquil green, is the starting point for a gentle meander through the Stour Valley with its namesake river keeping you company for much of the way. A well laid out path – the Great Stour Way – makes this walk a real pleasure. For a longer option there is an extension right into the heart of the ancient and world-renowned city of Canterbury, a place famous for both medieval pilgrims and 21st-century tourists.

> **Terrain:** Very gentle gradients between points 1 and 2, otherwise flat throughout. A short distance of road walking in the village, then paths through fields. Beyond point 3 there is a well made up riverside path which also serves as a cycle route.
>
> **Livestock & Stiles:** Potential for cattle on riverside sections. Three stiles at the time of writing.
>
> **Dog Friendly?** Yes. At the time of writing there were no padlocks on the gates beyond point 1 and the stiles had work-around gaps for dogs.

THE ARTICHOKE looks as if it has come straight out of a film set as a designer's portrayal of the most ancient medieval hostelry imaginable, except this 700-year-old timber-framed building is the real thing. There's even an old well protruding through the floor. It's a Shepherd Neame house, the brewery which claims the longest continuing brewing heritage of any in the country. Yet the pub even outdoes that, claiming that a former landlord was brewing here in the 1650s. ☎ 01227 738316.

If you go for the extended walk, Canterbury has many pubs, cafés and restaurants to choose from.

The Walk

❶ From your parking spot head towards the church. Walk up Station Road away from the railway crossing, passing the village hall on the left, cross the river and pass the paper mill on the right. *The modern industrial building hides its history. The river provided power for a mill here nearly 1,000 years ago, although what function it served is not clear. It became a paper mill in 1730 and was water-powered until the 1950s.* Pass the Artichoke pub on the right then take the next footpath on the left. Go through the gate, walk a few metres along a tarmac drive then take the footpath straight across the field in front of you. At the end of the field, go through the two gates, keeping ahead along the tarmac track which skirts to the right of the house. In the same direction cross the next field, keeping to the side of the left-hand hedge line. Cross two stiles either side of a lane. Keep to the footpath initially next to the smaller set of electricity cables. After you have passed a small

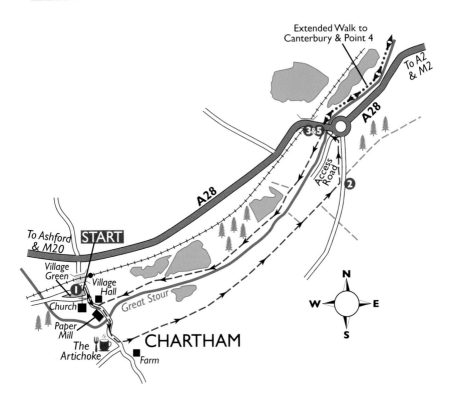

church on the other side of the hedgerow the exit from the field you are in will be a few metres to the right of the corner of the field. Don't go through the gate in the corner. Later the path will run straight across a grassy maintained meadow.

2 At the end of the meadow follow the path as it bears left parallel with the road below you on the other side of the hedge. Just before you get to the end, the footpath skirts the roundabout by going between the trees on your left. Cross the access road. Then bear slightly right across the grass, cross the stile next to the bridge to the far right-hand side of the tree line facing you. It is a little hidden.

3 For the 2½ mile route skip to point 5 on p16. If you want to take the much longer option into Canterbury, cross the road and drop down to the broad footpath ahead of you. This is the excellently

Westgate Gardens

maintained Great Stour Way which you follow, keeping the river always on your right-hand side, all the way to the cathedral city. Shortly after you have passed under the railway viaduct keep to the right avoiding the paths into the car park. After you have passed under the large road bridge turn right over the river at the next bridge into Westgate Gardens. Then turn left with the river now on your left following the path to the very end. You will see the towers of the Westgate through the trees ahead of you. The Westgate is – and has been for the last 600 years – the entrance to the medieval city of Canterbury.

4 Head down St Peter's Street, straight through the arch, the Cathedral is towards the end and a left turn down Mercery Lane. *It's impossible to condense into a few lines the attractions of Canterbury, suffice to say it was the birthplace of Christianity in England two thousand years ago, was walled by the Romans around AD 300 and is the seat of the Church of England. After the murder of Saint Thomas Becket at the hands of the King's knights at the cathedral in 1170, it became one of the most famous places in Europe,*

Waterside Walks in Kent

a place of pilgrimage from all parts of the Christian world and now a UNESCO World Heritage Site. To return to the walk, retrace your steps back to point 3. An alternative option, if you're flagging after a longer than intended walk around the city, is the train back to Chartham, just one stop from Canterbury West station, a very short distance back through the Westgate, (this would be the 4 mile option).

5 Back at point 3, turn left at the road, cross the bridge and then go through the first gate on the left-hand side and drop down to the river. This area is known as Milton Riverside and is claimed to be the best place to see kingfishers, although we were not so lucky! You now keep to the side of the Great Stour, following the Great Stour Way all the way back to Chilham village. *The Stour is a great example of a chalk river, notable for crystal-clear water, silt-free gravel beds and the home to water shrew and hereabouts, endangered water voles.* After a while the path becomes tarmac. The point in the river where the artificial mill channel joins the Great Stour is known as 'Tumbling Bay'. Keep following the path until it comes out onto the lane by the Village Hall, then turn right back towards the church and the village green.

Canterbury Westgate

Walk 3
EDENBRIDGE
3½ miles (5.6 km)

Start: Market Yard car park. **Sat Nav:** TN8 5BB.

Parking: There is a large free car park in the town centre, just off the High Street. Alternatively there is unrestricted parking in Cobbetts Way between points 1 and 2 on the walk.

Map: OS Explorer 147, Sevenoaks & Tonbridge.
Grid Ref: TQ444462.

This is a gentle meander through fields alongside a selection of small rivers and watercourses in the far west of the county. During this walk you will be alongside the Mill Stream, River Eden and the Kent Brook. This walk also takes in three officially named paths; The Eden Valley Walk, The Tandridge Border Path and the Vanguard Way.

The High Street, which you will walk down at the start and finish of the walk is well supplied with pubs and cafés. We particularly like **THE MINSTREL**, a small independent café using local suppliers located in a medieval timber-framed building at 86 High Street. ☎ 01732 863100. **THE SECRET CASK** at 91 High Street is in the best micropub tradition (not

---

Terrain: Mostly flat with one short very easy gradient. Stinging nettles may encroach the path in places between points 3 and 4 so avoid bare legs in summer.

Livestock & Stiles: Potential for livestock throughout. Several stiles.

Dog Friendly? Unfortunately not due to some wired stiles.

---

open Mondays). ☎ 07595 262247. Alternatively, stock up for a picnic from **COOKS THE BAKERY** (next to the bus stop on the right-hand side).

The Walk

1 From the town centre car park return to the High Street and turn left. Walk along the road until you get to the bridge over the River Eden. *It was the building of 'Eadenhelms bridge' in the 10th century that gave both the town and the valley their names. Today a selection of medieval buildings, coaching inns, courtyards, and the church flank the historic High Street, which is now by-passed by through traffic. The High Street is dead straight, being built along the course of the forgotten London to Lewes Roman road. The present single-arch stone bridge (dated 1836) replaced a six-arch design in stone first built in the reign of Henry VII.* Just before the bridge take the footpath on the right-hand side with the river on your left. A few metres later cross the road and take the opposite footpath just to the left of Cobbetts Way. Immediately turn right along the tarmac footpath keeping the houses on your right-hand side. When you get to the playing fields turn left, walk down the side of the playing fields keeping the tree line on your left. At the end cross the bridge.

2 Following the footpath marker number 614 keep ahead with the river on your left-hand side. This path is part of the Eden Valley Walk. Don't take the right-hand fork. Keeping the River Eden to your left, just over ½ mile later you get to a small bridge with a curious metal 90° gate/stile on the other side. Cross the little bridge, go through the stile and then keep ahead in the same direction. You are now facing an airstrip. *East Haxted Farm Airfield*

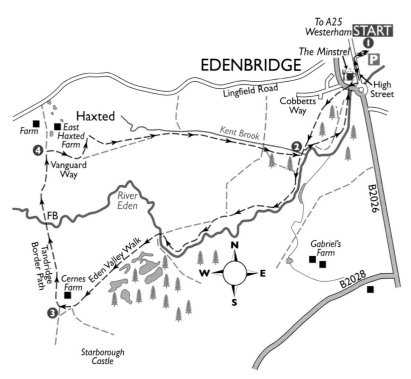

is part of a small private flying club that comprises four grass runways all differently orientated (and crossed by footpaths) to maximise its use by very small aircraft in a variety of conditions. Note the sign. Walk straight across the airstrip in the same direction keeping another pillbox on the left-hand side. A waymarker will soon confirm the route. Take the next left at the first bridge across the river. Then cross the small field in the same direction. Keep going straight ahead along a broad track first then a grassy track. When a further track bisects the route keep ahead along the public footpath over the stile into Cernes Farm. If in doubt of the route you will see a farmhouse ahead of you, the footpath emerges from the field next to the left-hand side of the farmhouse. Cross the little bridge and the stile and bearing slightly right a few metres later you will be out onto a broad track. If you wish to take in the surroundings of Starborough Castle turn left. *The brick building, currently a hotel and wedding venue, was built in 1870, but tucked behind it is an ancient, still water-filled moat dating back to the 1340s. Inside it once*

Crossing a runway

stood a medieval castle, dating from the same time and said to be very similar to famous Bodiam. It remains private property, and although a public footpath skirts the site on its west and south sides there is only a glimpse to be had of the moat.

3 Returning to the main walk, with Cernes Farm on your right, cross the track waymarked the Vanguard Way. Go over the little bridge and immediately after the gate turn right. Curve right around the farm keeping the barn on the right-hand side then follow the footpath through the small gate into the next field keeping the fence line on the right-hand side. You now just keep going in the same direction across several fields and over a few bridges. Keep ahead in the same direction until you come to the next footpath on the right. At this point Haxted farmhouse will be visible just across the next field.

4 Take the right-hand turn, still the Vanguard Way. After a while the footpath will bear left, but not into the first field you come to. At the top turn right. After a short distance, bearing left towards the bottom left-hand corner of the field, follow the path into the hedge line then through another metal gate. The path may be indistinct here, but that is the corner that you are heading for. You now follow this path in the same direction all the way back to Edenbridge, keeping to the right-hand side of the Kent Brook when you come to it. This will bring you back out to point number 2. Re-cross the bridge but now about 20 metres later turn right along the path into the hedge line. Keep ahead along this path ignoring any other paths bearing right or left until you come out at the river. Once you are at the river turn left along the riverbank path. This will return you back to the start.

The cattle screen

Walk 4
EYNSFORD, FARNINGHAM & HORTON KIRBY
8 miles (12.8 km)

Start: Eynsford Car Park, High Street. **Sat Nav:** DA4 0AN.

Parking: The public car park in the village opposite the church (free at the time of writing).

Map: OS Explorer 162 Greenwich & Gravesend.
Grid Ref: TQ540655.

A lengthier stroll taking in four riverside villages (each one with a pub), plus fields and water meadows alongside the River Darent. Bridges are also a recurring theme! Of course, the walk can be divided up into shorter sections between individual villages if you prefer.

THE MALT SHOVEL at Eynsford dates back to the 16th century with the refurbished restaurant and large main bar areas retaining original beams. ☎ 01322 862164. Part of the Vintage Inns chain, the 16th-century **LION HOTEL** at Farningham enjoys a prominent spot right on the river. Dogs allowed in the bar area and there is also plenty of outdoor seating in a marvellous location. ☎ 01322 860621. **THE CHEQUERS** is a few metres up the hill into the older part of the village. Dating

> **Terrain:** One steep gradient (miss out the loop around point 2 to avoid this), otherwise flat or easy gradients, footpaths or quiet roads. Can be muddy in winter.
>
> **Livestock & Stiles:** None encountered – apart from ostriches on the other side of a fence! One stile, crossing the railway line near Eynsford (miss out the loop around point 2 to avoid this).
>
> **Dog Friendly?** Yes, for small to medium-sized dogs.

from 1797, its eclectic décor includes murals depicting local scenes, two large candelabra and a suit of armour. ☎ 01322 865222. **THE BULL** at Horton Kirby is a proper village local and well worth a visit. Five real ales in top condition are usually on offer. Comfortable, friendly, unpretentious and thoroughly recommended. ☎ 01322 860341. **THE BRIDGES**, one of two pubs in South Darenth is right underneath the railway viaduct but apparently the name reflects the name of a previous landlord, not its location. Decorated with emergency service memorabilia it has a small garden by the river. ☎ 01322 860588.

The Walk

1 Turn right out of the car park and take the first right. *This will bring you straight to Eynsford's picturesque ford and medieval bridge.* Cross the bridge and take the riverside path rejoining the lane a short distance later. Continue along the lane, soon with water meadows on your left, home to a breed of pedigree highland cattle for many years. Continue under the imposing Victorian railway viaduct and keep along the lane until you get to the Roman Villa on the right-hand side. Take the footpath on the right immediately after the villa which will climb up the hillside.

2 Before you get to the top of the hill take the first footpath on the right, just before the hedgeline. It's worth a pause here. You will now have some spectacular views of the rolling countryside of the Darent Valley, a designated Area of Outstanding Natural Beauty. Cross the next lane and follow the footpath as it drops downhill. Take care crossing the railway line. Small or medium sized dogs should have no problem getting through the gap in the stile. Follow the path to the bottom of the hill and turn left. Then take the next left into Sparepenny Lane. Once you have passed the last of the houses, take the permissive path (waymarked the Darent Valley Path) on the right which runs parallel to the road but at a slightly lower level through the field. On your right across the valley you have some fine views of Eynsford Castle. *The massive walls are Norman and date from the 1080, but 300 years later the castle was abandoned.* Follow the path to the end, going through a gate and turning right into the lane at the top of some steps.

3 At the end of the lane in Farningham village turn right and walk down to the bridge over the river. *Two hundred years ago Farningham thrived on its agriculture and, surprisingly, its industry – **2** look at the large paper*

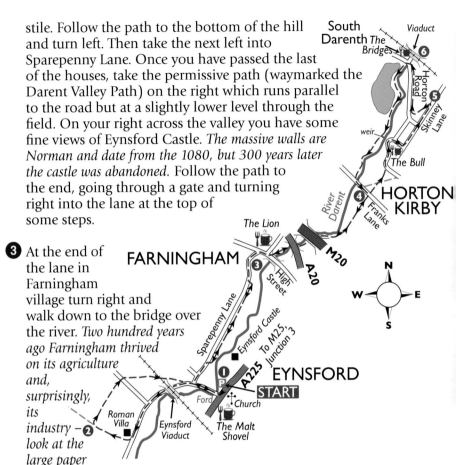

mill and fine Georgian house on the other side of the road from the pub. *Before the railways, six stagecoaches a day stopped in the village and one of the inns could stable 50 horses. The village has been a conservation area since 1969 (locally one of the first) and contains nearly 50 listed buildings.* Take the riverside path in front of the Lion Hotel with the river on your right-hand side. *You can't miss what looks like a quirky folly bridging the river. It's not a bridge, but a cattle screen, built around the mid-1700s when there was a ford here, to stop livestock wandering off down the river. Most screens were made from timber and were simple and functional. Why this one was so ornate is a mystery.* After a short distance cross the river over the footbridge, turn left and go underneath the road bridge. Continue ahead. After you've

Farningham Mill

gone under the second (motorway) bridge keep following the path bearing slightly right. The river will soon be on your left-hand side again. Continue along the path where it turns right, away from the river and follow it as it turns left.

4 Cross the lane and continue along the footpath straight ahead. Bear right at the gate at the end and then immediately left, keeping to the left-hand side of the field line. When you come out onto the lane, keep ahead along the road. Where the road bears right follow it and then keep going straight up the hill. At the top of the hill, with the Bull inn on the right, turn left. Follow the road out of the village. Once you have fields on both sides take the first footpath on the left. *To your right you can see the village of South Darenth and the 400ft-long Victorian railway viaduct dating from 1858.*

5 Follow the path to the bottom of the hill and take the dog-leg right, taking the path next to the lane but at a slightly higher level to it. Just before you get to the viaduct take the first left, passing the Bridges pub next to the arches. Cross the river.

6 Take the path on the left with the river now on your left. Continue along the riverside path. When you emerge onto playing fields keep to the left-hand fence line and pass to the left of the pavilion and toilets. If you divert a few metres along the access road you will get a view of the river tumbling over Horton Kirby weir. Cross the small car park and take the footpath at the far end. Continue along the Darent Valley Path. When you get to a lane turn left over the bridge. Continue along the lane a short distance and you'll be back at point 4. Turn right along the footpath and retrace your steps back to the start. At the Eynsford end of Sparepenny Lane just turn left to return to the car park. There is always The Plough on the left-hand side by the ford if you need another pub!

Ham Wharf

Walk 5
FAVERSHAM
2 miles (3.2 km)

Start: Upper Brents / The Albion Taverna. **Sat Nav:** ME13 7DR.

Parking: Unrestricted parking in Upper Brents road (follow the road as it bears right after the bridge) or a small 14-space car park by the Albion Taverna.

Map: OS Explorer 149 Sittingbourne & Faversham.
Grid Ref: TR015617.

This is a walk of contrasts; the route takes you away from the bustle of Faversham's historic quayside, through farmland and then marshes out to the remote and lonely waterside of Oare and Faversham creeks. The walk then follows Faversham Creek right back into the town using the Saxon Shore Way long-distance footpath.

THE ALBION TAVERNA at the start of the walk enjoys an enviable position by the creek with outside seating for waterside views. Despite its traditional Kentish clapboard appearance, it promotes itself as a Mexican cookhouse and is

> **Terrain:** Flat paths, tracks and a very quiet road. Sometimes the paths can be uneven.
>
> **Livestock & Stiles:** Cattle on the approach to point 4. No stiles.
>
> **Dog Friendly?** Yes.

certainly a good spot to while away some time. ☎ 01795 591411. The historic **SHIPWRIGHT'S ARMS** is near point 3 on the walk. Closed Mondays (except Bank Holidays). ☎ 01795 590088. There are also all manner of shops and cafés in Faversham town centre, a short distance from the start and finish of the walk.

The Walk

1 Start the walk at the creek side by Bridge Road bridge or by the Albion Taverna. Set off along the path with the creek on your right-hand side. On the other side of the creek you have views of some of the town's most historic buildings. *If the wind is blowing in the right direction, and you are getting an aroma of hops and malt, then brewing is taking place at Shepherd Neame, England's oldest brewery, with brewing on the site claimed to go back to the 1550s. The low waterfront timber-frame warehouse dates from 1475. Further along is Standard Quay, the town's main commercial port from the 1500s until the 1990s. Parts of it remain as working moorings as well as being home to several historic ships and barges.* A short distance later the footpath next to the creek has been closed. Take the path around the houses following the Ham Marsh trail sign. Where it emerges in front of an industrial estate turn left then immediately take the signposted Saxon Shore Way footpath behind the fence on the right-hand side.

2 Once you are out in the fields, at the next divergence of paths, keep straight ahead in the direction of the electricity power lines in the distance. Follow the footpath through the fields. At the end, turn left down the concrete road through the farmyard passing barns on either side. At the end of the farmyard bear right along the quiet road ahead of you, ignoring the footpath sign across the field. Continue along this road right to the far end, again ignoring the right-hand road signposted to the

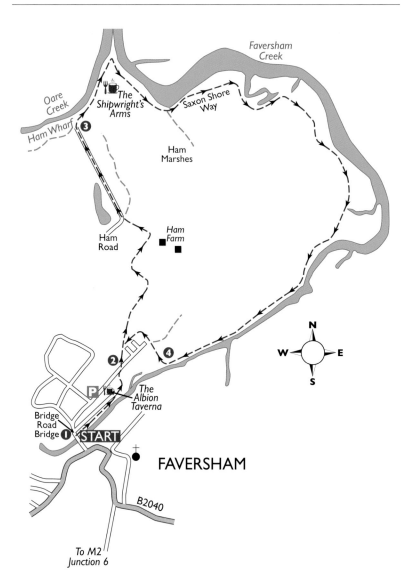

Shipwright's Arms. This will bring you out at Ham Wharf on Oare Creek.

❸ A few metres before you get to Ham Wharf, take the waymarked footpath on the right-hand side through the bushes with the creek on your left. You will soon pass the Shipwright's Arms on the right, and a few metres later you will come out at the head of the creeks. *The pub was first licensed in 1738 with parts of the building said to date back to the 13th century. At one time it claimed to be the haunt of Dutch smugglers. Sailors and fishermen in the Thames Estuary would stop off here before continuing up the creek to Faversham to unload. Testers Boatyard on the left continues the tradition of wooden boat building. This remote spot is known as Hollowshore. Once this was the seashore, hence the name, but over time the land*

has both silted naturally and has been drained by man for agriculture, a process started by the monks of Faversham Abbey. This part of the marsh is known by birdwatchers for its variety of birdlife, with some of the rarer species being spotted especially during migration periods. Follow the footpath round, keeping the water on your left-hand side. You now follow the Saxon Shore Way back into Faversham, keeping the creek on your left-hand side. Continue as far as you can alongside the creek. You will eventually be opposite the quays again. *The distinctive brick-built warehouse, although named Oyster Bay House on its town-facing side, has no historical link with oysters, despite the industry having flourished hereabouts and the Faversham Oyster Company (incorporated in 1180) being England's oldest company. The warehouse was built for the shipment of hops to London.*

4 When you are back at the first houses in Faversham you will encounter the footpath diversion again. Skirt the houses, keeping them on the left, go through the gate back to point 2 and retrace your steps to the start.

Walk 6
FOLKESTONE
5 miles (8 km)

Start: Marine Parade. **Sat Nav:** CT20 1SU.

Parking: Park in Marine Parade, some spaces are free between September and April. If there are no spaces there is a car park at the far end. The car park at the harbour itself is expensive for a longer stay.

Map: OS Explorer 138, Dover, Folkestone & Hythe.
Grid Ref: TR230357.

This walk starts in the rejuvenated area of Folkestone's seafront and, after a meander around the harbour, it takes you right up to the top of the iconic White Cliffs to the inspiring Battle of Britain Memorial. Here you can take in stunning views across the English Channel – on a clear day you should be able to see France.

The Stade, which you pass in both directions, has a number of pubs, we'd recommend **THE HARBOUR INN** at 24 Harbour Street ☎ 01303 487260, and a good café, the **CAPTAIN'S**

> **Terrain:** Plenty of variety; some walking on a roadside tarmac path, otherwise harbour-side streets, a promenade, as well as grassy, tarmac and cliff top paths; a boardwalk across the beach and a wander down to the end of the harbour arm and back. It's uphill, long and steady from the harbour to the views from the cliff top.
>
> **Livestock & Stiles:** None encountered. No stiles.
>
> **Dog Friendly?** Yes.

TABLE ☎ 07427 595933. There is a fish and chip shop on the right-hand side of the big hotel. **THE VALIANT SAILOR PUB** is just off the walk at the top of the cliffs ☎ 01303 250737. The **COCKPIT CAFÉ** is upstairs at the Battle of Britain Memorial, but does not allow dogs. Lots of independent eateries in season on the harbour arm. Check ⊕ folkestoneharbourarm.co.uk

The Walk

❶ Walk back along Marine Parade until you get to the Inner Harbour. Turn left with the large hotel on your left-hand side and the inner harbour on your right-hand side. *Although the first harbour here was built during the reign of Henry VIII, who visited the town in 1543, the one you see today was the work of renowned engineer Thomas Telford and was completed in 1810. Its importance took off in 1842 when the South Eastern Railway, having bought the harbour out of dereliction, turned Folkestone into the principal cross-channel sea port for Boulogne.* Walk around the harbour side. Keep the square and the Royal George pub on your right-hand side, cross Beach Street and then take the first right into The Stade. Take the left-hand turn by the Captain's Table café and go up the steps immediately ahead of you. At the top follow around to the right past the school and the church until you get to the grassy area at the top.

❷ Keep to the right-hand side of the grassy area and when you get to the residential road (Wear Bay Road) bear right along the path next to the road. Follow the road as it bends left past the East Cliff Pavilion up towards the top. *The East Cliff itself was given to the local council by landowner Lord Radnor in 1924 to improve*

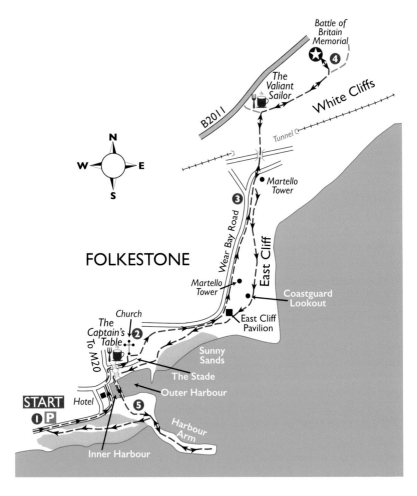

the amenities of the town. In 1934 the council opened the pavilion to provide a dance hall and restaurant. It was the first building in Folkestone to be heated and lit exclusively by electricity. Once you are beyond the golf course you can walk up the green.

3 Where the road bears left, keep ahead up the access road to the campsite (just by the second Martello Tower). Where the road to the campsite bends right, take the footpath uphill straight ahead. You will now be climbing to the top of the cliffs. At the top turn right. (If you miss the turn you'll soon come out onto the main

Battle of Britain Memorial

road at the Valiant Sailor pub. Useful if you need a pint.) Having turned right, follow the path as it climbs up to the clifftop. Turn left along the cliff path, following the North Downs Way sign. Don't take the right-hand path back downhill, continue along the clifftop path until you get to the Battle of Britain Memorial on your left, which is well worth a visit. *As well as a replica Spitfire and Hurricane there is a striking full-size stainless steel sculpture of a grounded Junkers Ju 87. The entire ground plan is centred on a large propeller shape, making the memorial as striking from the air as it is from the ground.*

4 Having taken time to explore, retrace your steps. When you are back just before point 3 take the footpath on the left and drop back down the grassy path to the left of the golf course with sea views across East Wear Bay. Head for the old Coast Guard lookout on the brow of the hill and then drop back down towards the town. When you have passed the East Cliff Pavilion take the first footpath on the left-hand side which drops back down towards the sea. Walk down the steps and turn right along the top of Sunny Sands promenade. Follow it round to the outer harbour on your left-hand side. *In the 19th century, while other parts of Folkestone became fashionable, this quayside remained a warren of hovels, fish markets, sail lofts, net-drying sheds, chandlers and pubs. Smuggling was rife as it was much more profitable for experienced sailors than fishing. Back in 1746 a Royal Commission stated that 6 tons of tea and 1,000 gallons of* *brandy were smuggled into Folkestone each week.* Go underneath the arches at the far end, then turn sharp left and go up the steps onto the old viaduct that crosses the harbour. Cross the bridge to the far end and keep ahead along the platforms of the former Folkestone Harbour Station to where the platform canopy finishes on the right-hand side and there is a ramped gap in the platform.

5 If the harbour arm is open, go through the gates ahead to the far end, loop up the stairs behind the lighthouse and return along the higher level. *See if you can find the hidden Iron Man sculpture by Sir Antony Gormley.* Take the boardwalk from the gap in the platform across the beach. This will bring you back to Marine Parade and the start of the walk.

Sunny Sands Beach

Walk 7
FOOTS CRAY MEADOWS

2½ miles (4 km)

Start: Foots Cray Meadows car park. **Sat Nav:** DA14 5PB.

Parking: At the time of writing the car park was free of charge. If full, there is plenty of unrestricted parking on the side roads just off the North Cray Road (close to point 4 on the walk if you need to use it as an alternative).

Map: OS Explorer 162, Greenwich & Gravesend.
Grid Ref: TQ473715.

This is a walk through woods, water meadows and alongside the River Cray in the grounds of what were once the private estates of two Elizabethan manor houses and are now a local nature reserve. In the 18th century the entire area was landscaped by the legendary Lancelot 'Capability' Brown.

Sidcup High Street has a variety of cafés and pubs for every taste, from individual coffee shops to a Wetherspoon's pub. Return back down Rectory Lane and turn right at the traffic lights. The High Street is at the top of the hill. Car parks are a left

> **Terrain:** Mostly flat with very easy gradients. Footpaths and a short distance on a tarmac drive. In winter you will get better views of the river which tend to be more obstructed by growth in the summer.
>
> **Livestock & Stiles:** None encountered. No stiles.
>
> **Dog Friendly?** Yes, very popular with dog walkers.

turn at the next crossroads at the end. There is some unrestricted parking at the far end of some of the side roads on the right-hand side. A good alternative less than a mile away, and one of our favourites, is the **HANGAR MICROPUB** at 37 The Oval, DA15 9ER. ☎ 0208 300 6909.

The Walk

1 Turn left out of the car park following the wildlife and information centre sign, walk up the drive with Foots Cray Place stables on the left-hand side. *The stable block, with its walled garden, was built in 1856 and was a service building for Foots Cray Place.* Keep along the driveway and then the tarmac path. At the second entrance into the park and information board, head into the park and follow the path. *Look for the large brick gatepost still standing in*

FOOTS CRAY
MEADOWS

Footbridge 3

Riverside
Woodland

Old
Gatepost

North Cray
Woods

Site of
Foots Cray
Place

Stable
Block

Lime
Avenue

Five Arch
Bridge

4

St James
Church

START

P 1

N
W E
S

Foots Cray
Lawns

Rectory Lane

All Saints
Church

Penny Farthing
Bridge 5

To Sidcup

Sidcup
Hill

Cray Road

To A20
& M25
Junction 3

the undergrowth on the right-hand side. Foots Cray Place stood on the right-hand side beyond the trees. The original manor is mentioned in the Domesday Book and at one stage belonged to the Walsingham family. Sir Francis Walsingham famously established a spy network for Queen Elizabeth I which uncovered the Babington Plot and led to the execution of Mary, Queen of Scots. In 1754, a new house was commissioned and became one of only four country houses in England built to an Italian Palladian design – a central domed core surrounded on each side by massive, full-height porticos. This magnificent mansion was sadly demolished in 1950 after a fire the previous year. At the T-junction of paths bear right. Now head slightly downhill through the woods and follow the path where it bears left at the end with the meadows now on the right-hand side.

Waterside Walks in Kent

2 Cross the tarmac path and then take the left-hand path into the field keeping the tree line on your left-hand side. Follow the path around the far left-hand corner of the field. At the next tree line turn left. Now take the right-hand path at the fork which will head into the trees ahead. At the end keep right with the children's playground on the left-hand side. Follow either fork of the path keeping the river on your right-hand side.

3 Cross the narrow footbridge. At the end turn immediately right. Now keep ahead with the river on the right-hand side at all times. At the diagonal crossroads of paths bear right. This will bring you out at Five Arch Bridge. *This is the centerpiece of the landscaping of the meadows carried out by Capability Brown in the 1780s. His own account book shows that he was paid nearly £2m in today's money for the work. He reshaped the River Cray to create the ribbon-like lake and designed the Five Arch Bridge, which was mainly brick and included a weir on its north side. He also landscaped the parkland, making a series of walks and drives around the estate.*

4 After the bridge, continue in the same direction with the lake on your right-hand side. Further ahead keep to the right-hand side track.

5 Cross the river at the next bridge, this is known as the Penny Farthing Bridge. Take the left, then right-hand fork and then bear left keeping the church spire behind the trees on your left-hand side. Keep alongside the perimeter of the park and follow the path along the avenue of chestnut trees. This will bring you back to the start.

Walk 8
GREATSTONE & THE SOUND MIRRORS
6 miles (9.7 km)

Start: Marine Parade, Littlestone. **Sat Nav:** TN28 8NP.

Parking: When you get to the seafront there is some unrestricted parking in Marine Parade or alternatively a pay and display car park off Grand Parade.

Map: OS Explorer 125, Romney Marsh, Rye & Winchelsea. **Grid Ref:** TR083238.

This is a walk brimming with atmosphere and modern history, taking you through a unique landscape of shingle and sand that edges up against the only official desert in the United Kingdom, part of which is also a nature reserve. Along the way you'll also encounter three historic (but little known) structures of international significance. If at all possible, do the walk at low tide as there is more to see and it gives you a chance to take in a long stretch on the beach. The route can be shortened by using car parks further along the coast road.

This is the English seaside and the coast road towards Greatstone has a number of cafés and fish and chip shops, or if you are looking for something else New Romney High

> **Terrain:** Other than short climbs over or up to the dunes it is billiard table flat – hundreds of years ago all this was beneath the sea. Apart from a couple of extremely quiet residential roads you will be on paths or on the beach. However some of the walk is on shingle which is more challenging and you may like to factor this in when considering timescales for completing the walk.
>
> **Livestock & Stiles:** Nothing four-legged encountered but be aware you will be walking through a RSPB bird reserve. No stiles.
>
> **Dog Friendly?** Yes, subject to care and caution on RSPB land. There are notices showing where dogs must be on leads.

Street (TN28 8AZ) has more variety. Locally renowned for fresh fish and usually open at lunchtimes and early evening is the **BRITANNIA INN** at Dungeness (TN29 9ND), which is a short distance further along the coast near the lighthouse. ☎ 01797 321959. **LADE STORES**, on the walk, is useful for some basics to eat on the beach.

The Walk

1 From wherever you have parked, face the sea and turn right. To start with you can follow the beach or the dunes, although there will be a few places where you are restricted to the beach. Continue past the lifeboat station.

2 Look out for the big new modern grey residential house and the point where the coast road dips back to run next to the sea. Here you will very soon draw level with Seaview Road down on your right-hand side. (If you've got as far as the footpath sign marked England Coast Path alternative route and the entrance to Romney Sands Holiday Park, you've gone a little bit too far. Just double back along the coast road and Seaview Road will now be on your left.) Walk down Seaview Road to the far end, then take the footpath ahead. Cross the strip of shingle, walk to the lake and then turn left along the footpath. *The lakes form part of Lade Pits, a restored gravel quarry which was handed over to the RSPB in 2015 and now forms part of their RSPB Dungeness Nature Reserve. This area of vegetated shingle, fen, reed bed and open water,*

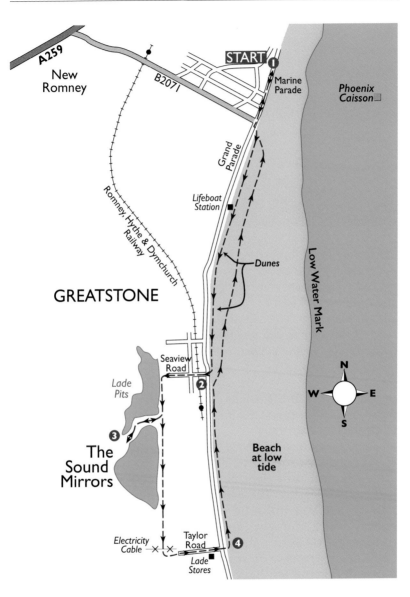

is home to marsh harriers, great white egrets, medicinal leeches and the rare Sussex emerald moth. The first footpath on the right will be the entrance to the sound mirrors. It's well worth the diversion to get an impressive closer look. Looking like something from a retro sci-fi

movie, the sound mirrors are massive concrete structures built between 1928 and 1930 as an early warning system for Britain to detect enemy aircraft. There were three designs of mirrors, 20ft, 30ft, and 200ft, and all three can be seen here. The concave surface picked up distant aircraft noise which was focused onto a collecting microphone (which can still be seen in the middle of the 30ft mirror). They did work, but were almost immediately rendered obsolete by the development of radar from 1935.

3 At the end of the shingle causeway there is an observation point. Direct access across the final watercourse is usually barred to protect the structures from graffiti vandalism. *There are very occasional open days organised by the RSPB – check www.rspb.org.uk/ reserves-and-events/reserves-a-z/dungeness.* Return along the single causeway and turn right at the end along the same footpath you were on earlier. The path here is along the course of an old railway line. You will soon see one of the bridges that took the railway over a footpath. Once you have walked past the length of the lakes on your right, and very shortly after you have gone underneath the set of small electricity cables, take the next footpath on your left-hand side. Like all public footpaths across the Dungeness shingle it is very indistinct. *The vast expanse of shingle forming into a headland at Dungeness has led to claims that it qualifies as a desert. It is of international conservation importance for its plant, invertebrate and bird life. It is an eerie, otherworldly place with wooden shacks (several of which have been converted into luxury* *retreats), two nuclear power stations, two lighthouses (only one of each in use), stunted plants and the discarded rusting remains of the fishing industry.* Cross the shingle to where the line of the electricity cables you have just walked under meets the road. Walk to the end of the road. The remains of Lade Fort are a few metres along Lade Fort Crescent on the right. Lade Stores on your right is an ideal point to buy anything you might want for a snack on the beach. At the end of the road you'll be back out onto the seafront.

4 Turn left and head back to Littlestone. Again you have the choice of the coast road, the shingle ridge or the beach and later parts of the dunes. When you get close to Littlestone, and if the tide is low enough, look out to sea at the large rectangular concrete structure in the water with navigation lights on each corner. *It doesn't look like much from here but this Phoenix Caisson is of greater historical importance than the sound mirrors. It is a Second World War floatable harbour component. In 1944 the allies landed on a part of the French coast which had no significantly large harbour. Two were needed, so incredibly they were built as prefabricated parts in Britain and two entire harbours were floated across the English Channel. The caissons, used to create outer breakwaters, were deliberately sunk before being needed to avoid being seen by German reconnaissance. This one got stuck in the silt and couldn't be re-floated.*

Walk 9
GROVE FERRY & STODMARSH
3 miles (4.8 km)

Start: Grove Ferry Picnic Site. **Sat Nav:** CT3 4BP.

Parking: At Grove Ferry Picnic Site public car park. There is no credit card reader on the machines so bring change.

Map: OS Explorer 150 Canterbury & Isle of Thanet.
Grid Ref: TR236631.

This is a watery walk through the national nature reserve at Stodmarsh, finishing with a walk along the Great Stour. The reserve is formed of internationally important reed beds, fens, ditches, wet grassland and open water, which provide an ideal habitat for breeding and wintering birds, invertebrates and rare plants. This site is especially important for bittern and marsh harriers, plus rarer inhabitants including the shining ramshorn snail and water vole. A tip for this walk is to try it in winter, provided you are happy to get a bit muddy! The bird population is greater and there are better views of the watercourses and the river.

> **Terrain:** Flat waymarked paths either tarmacked or grassy – muddy in winter!
>
> **Livestock & Stiles:** Nothing large and four-legged but an abundance of birds and small animals as it's a nature reserve. No stiles.
>
> **Dog Friendly?** Dogs are welcome in most areas of the reserve if they are on a lead, but not on the signposted 'Short Circuit Nature Trail' and the 'Nature Trail Extension' which are not part of the main walk.

THE GROVE FERRY INN is next to the car park at the start and finish of the walk. Open from 11am daily it has a large riverside garden. ☎ 01227 860302. Seasonally, there is a street food mobile café in the car park.

The Walk

1 Exit the car park and turn right at the lane. A few metres later turn left down the first footpath. Follow the broad track which will become grassy after a time. There will be bird hides and observation points on either side of this landscape of marshes, ponds, channels and lily-filled watercourses. *The ditches allow water circulation around the reserve and provide a habitat for a range of rare plants such as sharp-leaved pondweed and rare invertebrates including the shining ramshorn snail. The water levels are controlled to stop them drying up and are cleared out periodically to prevent them becoming choked with reeds or scrub.* Once you cross a footbridge, you will come out at a T junction of paths.

2 Turn right and then immediately left. Keep ahead. The path will cross an unmade track, head slightly diagonally right across it. Again keep going in the same direction. Once you have passed Marsh Hide on the right, the path will bear 90° left, follow it round. *In medieval times the monks from Canterbury dug the first ditches to bring river water into the meadows. Horses were grazed and the area was first known as Stud marsh. In contrast to today, in the 1930s the marshes were used for duck shooting.* Keep following the path as it turns. After a while Undertrees Farm will be visible through the trees on the left-hand side.

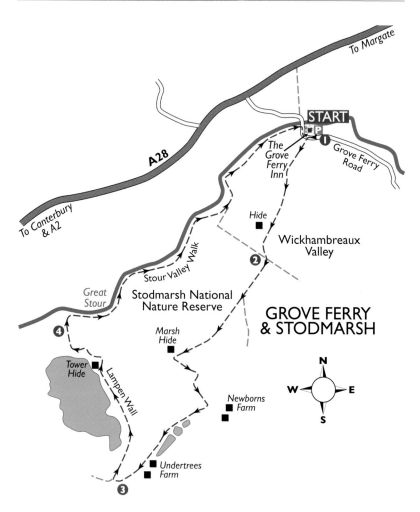

GROVE FERRY & STODMARSH

3 Eventually you will come out at the junction of paths close to a wooden commemorative bench. Bear right, don't cross the footbridge. Ignore the first footpath on the right marked 'nature trail'. At the T-junction now a few metres ahead of you, turn right along the broad track, following the red arrow nature reserve waymarker. You are now on the raised Lampen Wall, an 18th-century flood defence barrier, with its water channel on your left. Soon you will have views across one of the lakes to the right. The next turn on the right is a bridge over some ponds which is the reserve's nature trail. *That Kent had a substantial coalfield is a surprise to many people. Coal was extensively mined; the pits were in a triangle bounded by Canterbury, Ramsgate and Dover. One of the collieries was at nearby Chislet, which opened in 1914 and its underground workings stretched out to what is now the nature reserve. This caused the land to slightly subside and become the*

waterlogged landscape you see today. Chislet closed in 1969, whilst the last pit in the coalfield, at Betteshanger, lasted until 1989. It is estimated there are still 100 million tons of coal beneath East Kent. You can take this short circular diversion that will bring you back out near point 3 to return to the walk. Pass the Tower bird hide on the left and continue along the path.

4 After a short while the broad Great Stour joins the path on the left-hand side. You now follow this leisurely riverside walk all the way back to Grove Ferry. When the path emerges behind the moorings out onto the road, turn right and the car park is a few metres further on your left-hand side, just the other side of the Grove Ferry Inn.

Walk 10
KEARSNEY
2½ miles (4 km)

Start: Alkham Road car park. **Sat Nav:** CT16 3EE.

Parking: The car park is just by the pedestrian crossing opposite Russell Gardens on Alkham Road.

Map: OS Explorer 138, Dover Folkestone & Hythe.
Grid Ref: TR285437.

There is plenty of variety in this walk, which starts and finishes in formal gardens and landscaped parkland around the River Dour, but also takes you up into the hills overlooking the Alkham Valley. Dover may be famous as the gateway to England, but the river from which it gets its name, the Dour, is one of Kent's forgotten rivers and is only four miles long.

There is a café in what used to be the west wing and billiard room of **Kearsney Abbey** – the only part of the original Victorian building left standing. The café is at point 4 on the walk and features a terrace overlooking the parkland and Abbey Lake.

> **Terrain:** A variety of paths, tracks and a quiet country lane through landscaped parkland, woods and fields. One significant lengthy uphill gradient of ¼ mile.
>
> **Livestock & Stiles:** None encountered, but be aware of waterfowl. No stiles.
>
> **Dog Friendly?** Yes.

The Walk

1 Cross the road at the traffic lights, go through the gate opposite and bear left past the pavilion up to the broad ornamental canal. This is Russell Gardens – take some time to explore. *Russell Gardens takes its name from a former mayor of Dover who was instrumental in saving the gardens as a public open space. Formerly the private grounds of Kearsney Court, the garden, water features, long canal pond, and waterfalls beneath the Palladian-style pergola bridges were created using the flow of the River Dour by the Edwardian landscape architect, Thomas H. Mawson.* Continuing the walk, keep to the left-hand side of the canal, following the path through the next pavilion. At the end, cross the bridge and bear left. Climb gently up to the next lake which you now cross by the weir. *Bushy Ruff Lake was created in the 1820s when the Dour was dammed to feed two mills. It became a publicly open extension to Russell Gardens in the 1970s, its wilder informal nature being a contrast to the formal gardens downstream.* Then, keeping to the left-hand side of the lake, continue through the grassy area past the benches and take the path ahead through the trees. Take the next dogleg right at the litter bin. Then immediately the dogleg left following the

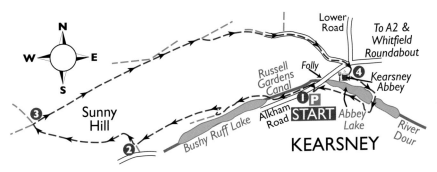

path out of the trees and through the gate into the field. Keep to the permissive path on the left-hand side of the field to the far end. Towards the end it will become a track.

2 Bear right at the end and follow the track steeply up the side of the hill. There are great views of the Alkham Valley behind you. The track will climb on through some woods, when you emerge from the trees at the top of the hill, go through the gate ahead of you. Immediately turn sharp right following the yellow waymarker. At this stage do not follow the Kearsney loop sign.

3 Keep the treeline of the large field to your immediate right. At the far end, go through the first (more hidden) gate in the right-hand treeline. Keep ahead where the tracks merge. Now keep to the red waymarked Kearsney Loop path passing some cottages on the right. The path will become a track and later a narrow tarmac lane. Follow this steeply right down to the very end, ignoring the footpath on the left-hand side. Keep going right down to the very bottom. At the end, cross the road bearing slightly left and then go through the gateposts in the park wall. Note the old doorways either side. The café and terrace with its views of the ornamental lake is on the right. *The café is all that remains of Kearsney Abbey. It was never an abbey in the religious sense, the* *name abbey was sometimes just given to add perceived grandeur to a large private house – Downton Abbey is a good, if fictitious, example. Kearsney was built in the 1820s, but notably reused material from medieval town walls and gatehouses which were being demolished in Dover at the time – including, quite spectacularly, one of the round towers from the harbour that featured in Henry VIII's departure to the Field of the Cloth of Gold in 1520. Incredibly it was all lost in the 1960s when most of it was pulled down due to dry rot in some of the timbers. Not even the Tudor tower was spared, only lingering on in isolation for a short while until it was said to have been sold for just £2,000 to a demolition contractor for reclamation of the 'debris'. Only the billiard room – then a tea room and now the café – survived. Even the landscaped parkland was earmarked as an overflow parking lot for cross-channel cars and caravans. However the area is now safe with both Grade II listing status and a recent £3.3m lottery-funded 'Parks for People' grant.*

4 Take the path down to the lakeside. Don't cross the first bridge, keep to the path to the left of the lake. Cross the bridge at the end of the lake. Follow the path round past the high brick wall on your left, a few metres later turn right, Then bear immediately left back towards the car park. *A few metres from the car park, along the path on the right, are the remains of an ornamental mock ruin and waterfall built across the stream and created when the grounds of the house were laid out. It is also built of material salvaged from medieval buildings demolished in Dover in the early 19th century, one stone is dated 1609.*

Walk 11
KESTON PONDS
2½ miles (4 km)

Start: Keston Fish Ponds Car Park. **Sat Nav:** BR2 6AT.

Parking: If Keston Fish Ponds car park is full there is an alternative in Heathfield Road (turn right and then second exit at the roundabout, car park on the left-hand side, BR2 6BF).

Map: OS Explorer 147, Sevenoaks & Tonbridge.
Grid Ref: TQ419639.

This walk starts at the very source of the River Ravensbourne, a place steeped in ancient history and legend. It passes several ponds created by damming the river in the little valley and explores the local beauty spot that has been established around them. The walk then heads out into the countryside to the Wilberforce Oak, a quiet almost forgotten spot where the momentous decision was made to abolish the slave trade in the British Empire. A short distance further on is the chance for a break at a local farm shop café or tea garden.

HOLWOOD FARM CAFÉ is at point 5 on the walk. Holwood was a working farm until quite recently – morning commuters in their cars would have to wait in Shire Lane whilst the dairy

> **Terrain:** Moderate gradients in places. Only a few yards of road walking to access the café. Can be muddy.
>
> **Livestock & Stiles:** None encountered. No stiles.
>
> **Dog Friendly?** Yes.

cows were walked across the lane to the milking parlour. Some of its buildings have now been converted into a farm shop and café including an outside tea garden terrace. Closed Mondays. ☎ 01689 638381. Dogs allowed in the tea garden. Nearest pub is **THE GREYHOUND**, a CAMRA award winner which enjoys a great location right on the green at Keston village. Turn right out of the car park, sharp right at the roundabout then follow Heathfield Road down to the crossroads where you turn right at the green. ☎ 01689 856338.

The Walk

1 Take the footpath at the bottom end of the car park. Go down the steps and cross the well on the right. The modern brick finish is the surround to Caesar's Well. *Legend has it that in 54BC Julius Caesar and his invading Roman army came this way, heading inland having landed on the Kent coast. The legions needed to replenish their water supply and scouts ahead, seeing a pair of ravens, thought it might be a sign of fresh water. They were led to this spring (there never was, or has been a well) and made camp. The spring is the source of the River Ravensbourne, which takes its name from the legend.* Now bear left. Keep the pond on the left-hand side. There are several paths at different levels that will bring you out at Fishponds Road. When you get to Fishponds Road turn left, keeping the lake on your left-hand side, then take the public footpath first right. Head into the woods and then immediately bear right following the purple waymarker down to the next pond, taking the path by the water. At the end of this pond turn right again, following the purple waymarker and go over the little bridge at the end of the pond. At the end turn left and follow the path through the woods. Don't cross the next small bridge over the river but keep ahead. Continue on, passing another pond on the right-hand side and across a boardwalk. A few metres later the

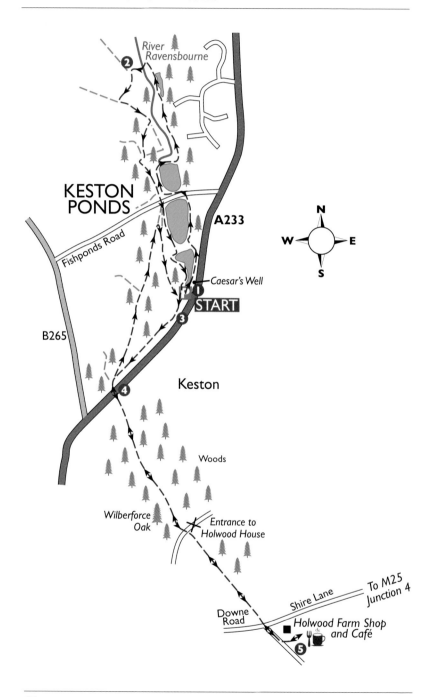

River
Ravensbourne

KESTON
PONDS

A233

Fishponds Road

Caesar's Well

START

B265

Keston

Woods

Wilberforce
Oak

Entrance to
Holwood House

Shire Lane

To M25
Junction 4

Downe
Road

Holwood Farm Shop
and Café

N
W · E
S

path swings left. Almost immediately you reach the bridge across the stream, cross it and follow the path as it swings back left with the stream now on your left-hand side.

2 Keep left into the small field. Now keep to the path with the treeline on the right-hand side. *The land around here has been relandscaped over the years, and at times, the river has been diverted to create further ponds. At one time it was owned by the sugar company Tate & Lyle and later by an oil exploration company. Since the 1980s the area you are walking through has been preserved and is now a designated Site of Special Scientific Interest.* At the end of the field turn left. When you come out into the next field, take the right-hand path. Bear right at the end and immediately take the left, parallel to the bridle path. At an immediate crossing of paths continue ahead. When you come back to Fishponds Road take the path on the lower level with the pond on your left. Keep ahead to walk around the right-hand side of the next pond. When you are back at Caesar's Well go back up the steps to the car park.

3 Cross the car park and take the footpath at the top left-hand side. Continue gently uphill. At the very top follow the left-hand footpath sign out onto the main road.

4 Take care crossing the road and carry on along the footpath ahead. This is the path signed to Downe FP2315 via Wilberforce Oak. After ¼ mile you pass the Wilberforce Oak. *In 1787 William Pitt, who lived at Holwood House, was Prime Minister and his friend, William Wilberforce, was a Yorkshire MP. That year Wilberforce's diary records "I well remember a conversation with Mr Pitt in the open air at the root of an old tree at Holwood, just above the steep descent into the Vale of Keston. I resolved to give notice, on a fit occasion in the House of Commons my intention to bring forward the abolition of the slave trade". He led the campaign against the British slave trade for 20 years until the enactment of the Slave Trade Act of 1807. The current thriving oak tree is a third generation of the original; grown from an acorn from a tree which itself was grown from an acorn of the original. The stone bench, commemorating Wilberforce, dates from 1862.* Continue ahead crossing the main drive into Holwood House. Keep ahead. When you come out onto a lane, cross it and now continue straight ahead along the lane facing you.

5 The coffee shop is in Holwood Farm a few metres ahead on your left-hand side. You now retrace your steps to point 4. Turn right, but now take the left-hand fork. This will bring you out above, and with views of, the second pond close to Fishponds Road again. Now follow the tight dogleg right and follow this path back to the start.

Walk 12
KINGSDOWN
5 miles (8 km)

Start: Dover Patrol Memorial car park. **Sat Nav:** CT15 6DT.

Parking: There is a free car park at the Dover Patrol Memorial. If this is full do not park in the part of Granville Road which is designated as private, you will have to make your way back further and return on foot. There is no space for parking in Hotel Road.

Map: OS Explorer 138 Dover, Folkestone & Hythe.
Grid Ref: TR373452.

One of our favourite walks, taking in the spectacular white cliffs of Dover, panoramic views across the Channel to France, and a quiet undisturbed inland valley tucked away behind the cliffs. The walk links two relatively unknown gems in Kent, the small bay at St Margaret's hemmed in by chalk cliffs on both sides and the laidback village of Kingsdown, which sprawls right onto its own shingle beach.

THE ZETLAND ARMS is a one-of-a-kind classic sitting right on the shingle beach at Kingsdown. In summer you can eat or drink on the pub's benches by the sea, or in winter you can

Waterside Walks in Kent

> **Terrain:** Country paths, a length along a traffic-barred lane, a short section of quiet road, shingle beach and a glorious section of the Saxon Shore Way coast path along the top of the cliffs. One steep set of steps to climb.
>
> **Livestock & Stiles:** None encountered. No stiles.
>
> **Dog Friendly?** Very much so, but the usual degree of control is needed to ensure safety on the cliff tops.

cosy up to a log fire with the sound of the sea in the background. Nautically themed, it's a Shepherd Neame tied house with their seasonal autumn Late Red ale particularly recommended on tap. No food service between 2.45 and 6pm. ☎ 01304 370114.

The Walk

1 From the car park and with your back to the sea take the footpath with the brown tourist waymarker 'Explore Saint Margaret's Front Line Britain trail' to the left of the memorial. *The memorial is one of a trio, one being across the Channel at Cap Blanc-Nez and, curiously, one in New York. They commemorate the service of personnel and craft which worked and fought in the English Channel during the First World War. Two thousand members of the patrol lost their lives. The 75ft-high Egyptian-style obelisk was unveiled in 1921.* Go through the gate and take the footpath straight ahead across Bockell Hill, just to the left of the National Trust sign. Cross the field,

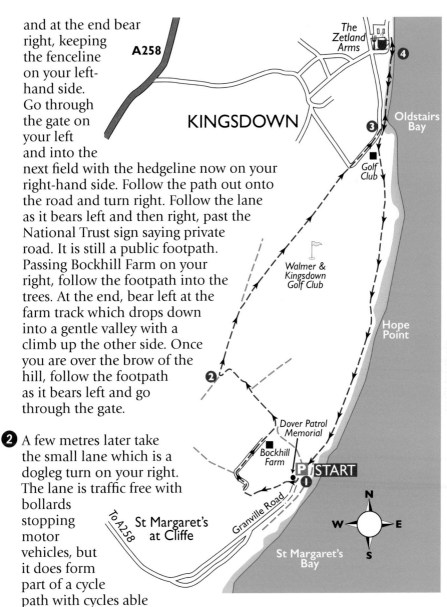

and at the end bear right, keeping the fenceline on your left-hand side. Go through the gate on your left and into the next field with the hedgeline now on your right-hand side. Follow the path out onto the road and turn right. Follow the lane as it bears left and then right, past the National Trust sign saying private road. It is still a public footpath. Passing Bockhill Farm on your right, follow the footpath into the trees. At the end, bear left at the farm track which drops down into a gentle valley with a climb up the other side. Once you are over the brow of the hill, follow the footpath as it bears left and go through the gate.

2 A few metres later take the small lane which is a dogleg turn on your right. The lane is traffic free with bollards stopping motor vehicles, but it does form part of a cycle path with cycles able to get up considerable speed on the long smooth downhill stretch. You now take this quiet traffic-free lane for 1½ miles right the way down the valley into Kingsdown. When you get to

the end bear left down the road and follow it right the way out to the seafront.

❸ When you get to the seafront turn left along the beach. You will see the houses of Kingsdown and, in particular, the legendary Zetland Arms pub ahead of you. Follow the beach around to the pub.

❹ Retrace your steps to point 3. Now take the set of steep steps up the cliff to the left of the road that you walked down earlier. It's waymarked Saxon Shore Way. Do not take the lower level path running along the base of the cliffs. At the top of the steps keep along the path passing the golf club on your right. If you turn round (on a clear day) you'll have great views looking back towards Kingsdown, Deal Pier and Thanet. You now just keep ahead along the coast path all the way back to the Dover Patrol Memorial. After you've passed the last of the houses on your right you'll see the memorial ahead of you on the skyline so you'll have no doubt in which direction you are heading! *One last surprise – you are now in original James Bond country. Author Ian Fleming had a weekend retreat in St Margaret's Bay and it was this landscape in particular that inspired him to write some of his novels. Legend has it that Bond's number 007 was chosen as that was the number of the express coach service from London to Dover, although it is highly unlikely that sports-car-driving Fleming would ever have been a passenger!*

Walk 13
LEYBOURNE
2 miles (3.2 km)

Start: Leybourne Lakes Country Park. **Sat Nav:** ME20 6JA.

Parking: At the main Country Park car park. The car park closes at dusk so check the times displayed on your way in.

Map: OS Explorer 148, Maidstone and The Medway Towns. **Grid Ref:** TQ696602.

This walk takes you around Leybourne Lakes Country Park, with nearly 100 hectares of lakes, grasslands, shallow wetlands, hedgerows and woodland, and the ridge of the North Downs in the background. Our route, as always, keeps to designated paths, but there are plenty of other informal paths maintained around the site if you want to explore further. Top tip – we wouldn't normally recommend this, but if you do this walk on a weekend when there will be plenty going on at the watersports centre, some of the activities such as windsurfing, kayaking, canoeing and diving will keep you entertained as you walk around. Of course, if you're after solitude, then weekdays during the winter are generally quiet and the lakes are also home to an over-wintering bird population.

Waterside Walks in Kent

> **Terrain:** Flat along established gravel or grassy footpaths. Some of the hard footpaths can be uneven in places.
>
> **Livestock & Stiles:** None encountered. No stiles.
>
> **Dog Friendly?** Very much so.

There is an onsite mobile café, although it is only a servery and seating is on outside picnic benches overlooking the lake. If you are hoping to use it, check it's open on your way past by following the signpost shortly after point 1 on the walk. If not, you can access a big Tesco between points 1 and 2 for either provisions or their own café. It has its own exit from the country park which has been noted on the map.

The Walk

1 With your back to the car park entrance, head to the left-hand side of the Rangers' office and toilet block. Follow the sign to the lakes. When you get to the watersports car park, follow the signpost for the watersports and café. Cross the wooden bridge and go straight ahead to the right-hand side of the green shipping

The Ocean

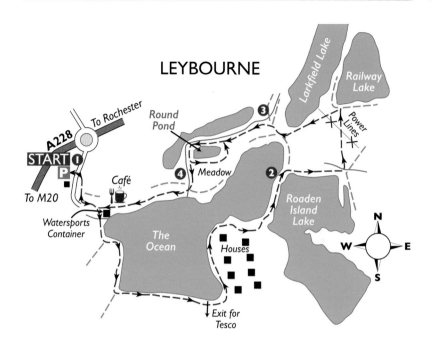

container. Keep following the path around the edge of the lake, keeping it on the left-hand side at all times. *This is the largest of the lakes, optimistically called The Ocean. All the lakes were once gravel pits but extraction finished in the 1980s. The pits then gradually flooded with water from a tributary of the nearby River Medway. They were landscaped and opened as a formal country park in 2004. Now the park is Natural England accredited, designated as a local wildlife site, and is a Green Flag Award winner.* After a while you pass a housing development on the right, with views back across the lake. Once you have passed the houses you will have water on both sides of the footpath as Roaden Island Lake joins on the right.

2 Where the paths diverge, just before a metal gate, keep to the right-hand path following the lake on the right. At the next T-junction of tracks turn left crossing the water ditch. Scrub and silt clearance has recently transformed this into a habitat for water voles, one of Britain's most dramatically declining mammals. Having crossed the ditch over the bridge, continue along the broad track towards the pylon. Once you have passed underneath the electricity wires

Round Pond

turn left along the track (to the right there is a viewing spot for the Railway Lake). Cross the small car park, and then cross over the small bridge and bear right.

3 Keep right following the sign for Brooklands and Neville Park, but then turn immediately left up a very slight bank on a grassy path. If you've reached a small bridge over a stream, retrace your steps a little as you've gone too far and missed the turn. Now follow the grassy path. The Round Pond (also used as a dipping pond) will soon be on your left behind the trees. Follow it round and you will come out into a wild flower meadow.

4 For better views of the Round Pond you can do a quick circuit around it, returning to this point. At point 4 continue ahead towards the main lake with the houses ahead of you slightly to the left. A few metres later, at the main path around the main lake, turn right. This will bring you to the café and the watersports shipping container. You now retrace your steps back to the car park.

Walk 14
LOWER HALSTOW
3 miles (4.8 km)

Start: Lapwing Drive, Lower Halstow. **Sat Nav:** ME9 7DZ.

Parking: Unrestricted parking in Lapwing Drive.

Map: OS Explorer 148, Maidstone and The Medway Towns.
Grid Ref: TQ858673.

On the edge of the Medway Marshes, this is a walk of two very different parts, half along country lanes flanked by fruit orchards, and half along the waterside Saxon Shore Way with the estuary of the River Medway for company. If possible, aim to do this walk at high tide, as there will be water closer to the path. At other times the water recedes to mudflats, which are not without their own charms. Check tide tables for Darnett Ness. Doing the walk in spring, when the orchards are in blossom, or late summer, when they're in fruit, is another bonus.

The village pub, Grade II listed **THREE TUNS**, was built in 1468 and has been licensed since 1764. There are smart dining and drinking areas inside and a large outdoor

> **Terrain:** Flat, country lanes or waymarked long distance footpath.
>
> **Livestock & Stiles:** None encountered. No stiles.
>
> **Dog Friendly?** Yes.

courtyard garden at the rear. Ales are from independent Kentish breweries (Old Dairy, Goachers and Wantsum on our last visit). The pub prides itself on using local produce, even down to fish when landed at nearby Queenborough. ☎ 01795 842840.

The Walk

1 Retrace your route back down Lapwing Drive to The Street (the main road through the village). Turn right and follow the road, passing The Green on the right-hand side. You soon leave the village and pass an old chapel on the right, and then the cricket green on the left. Take the next right down Twinney Lane. On your left you will have the first of many orchards that are a feature of the landscape here. *This area is part of a recognised 21-mile Kentish 'fruit belt', thanks to the fertile, well-drained soil. Henry VIII tasted new varieties of apples and pears in France and instructed*

Twinney Wharf

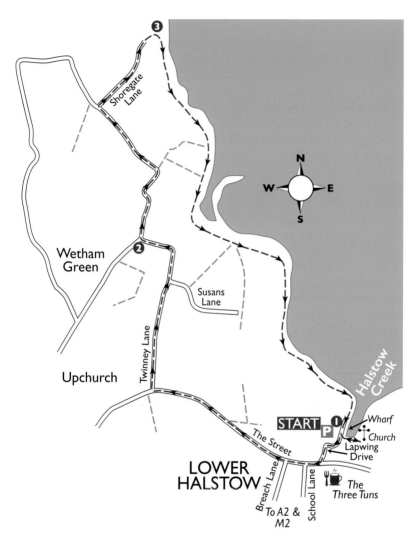

his gardener to replicate the different types. He brought trees back from France and in the 1530s, a few miles from here, on land given to him by the king, he set the seeds of what would become the fruit belt. It's still said to be one of the most productive agricultural areas in the county. Bear slightly left passing Susans Lane on the right. After a while you will have apple orchards to your left and pears to your right.

2 At the T-junction turn right following the sign for Ham Green. After you have passed Greylag Farm on the right and entered the hamlet of Ham Green, take the right-hand fork in the lane and turn right down Shoregate Lane.

3 At the boatyard gate turn right down the footpath, now following the Saxon Shore Way. The path curves round the boatyard. A few metres later, when you get to the estuary, follow the path right. On a clear day there some great views to be had across this wide estuary mouth of the River Medway. Ahead you can see the cranes of the international shipping terminal at London Thamesport (although it is on the Medway), and in the distance, to your right, the Kingsferry Bridge over the Swale channel. You now follow the Saxon Shore Way with the estuary on your left, passing through, and by, a few boatyards on the way. Most of the way you will still have orchards flanking the estuary path on the right-hand side. Just keep ahead and follow the path all the way back to Lower Halstow. *The village wharf here is home to the famous Thames sailing barge Edith May, built in Harwich, Essex, in 1906, to carry wheat and barley from East Anglia to London. After a period as a racing barge she became a museum ship in Liverpool and later London. In 1999 she returned to the Thames and now offers leisure trips on the River Medway. If you are lucky, at certain times she is open at the wharf as a tea room. The area around and behind the wharf was once a brick works. In 1912 it employed 120 men and boys and produced between 17 and 18 million bricks a year. The works closed in 1966 and its buildings were demolished but you can still see bricks embedded in the ground.* If you want to look at the ancient parish church, turn left at the end of the wharf along the short footpath. Parts of it date from 8th-century Saxon times, with reused Roman masonry. Later parts are from the 12th and 13th centuries. Returning down the short footpath will bring you back to Lapwing Drive and the start of the walk.

Halstow Creek

Walk 15
MOTE PARK
2½ miles (4 km)

Start: School Lane. **Sat Nav:** ME15 8DU.

Parking: There is a small car park on School Lane, at the time of writing the charging period starts at 10am, but is £2 for the whole day. Alternatively there is unrestricted parking on School Lane or Oxford Road opposite the entrance.

Map: OS Explorer 148, Maidstone and The Medway Towns. **Grid Ref:** TQ782542.

It's surprising how many people are unaware of the attraction of Mote Park, an 18th- and 19th-century landscaped park, right in the middle of Maidstone, Kent's county town. For a town park it stretches to an incredible 450 acres. Once a country estate, it became a public park in the 1930s. In the late 1790s the River Len, which runs through it, was dammed to create an enormous ornamental lake, which features in this waterside walk. The park is open from 8am until dusk.

The main park café is run by the borough council and is at point 3 on the walk with a refreshment kiosk (limited opening) near point 2.

Terrain: Mostly tarmacked drives and paths, all traffic free. A steep gradient down and corresponding climb back up at the start and end of the walk.

Livestock & Stiles: None encountered. No stiles.

Dog Friendly? Yes, very.

The Walk

❶ Take the path at the far end of the School Lane car park. Keep to the tarmac path as it drops down the hill. At the bottom bear left. Cross the River Len and follow the path as it starts to head uphill. *This is the less busy part of the park and, as you look around, you can appreciate the landscaping that took place 200 years ago. Going back further, it is thought this was one of the oldest deer parks in Kent.*

❷ *High on your right-hand side you will see Mote House, the park's stately home, built between 1793 and 1800 and now used as a retirement home.* Take the path a few metres further ahead on

Mote House

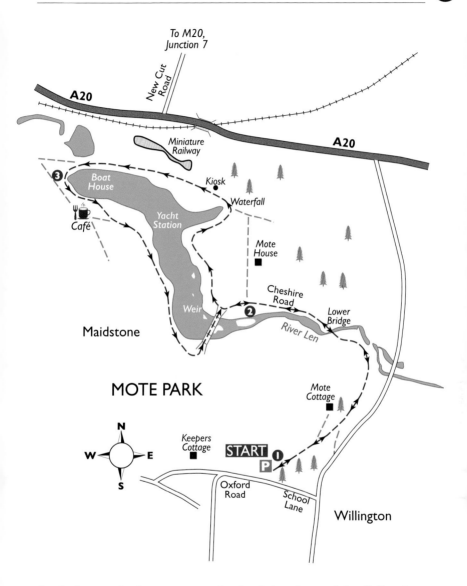

the left. Just before you reach the lake, bear right following the sign to the historic waterfall and ice cream kiosk. At the very end of this path turn left over the bridge which crosses the waterfall. Follow the path with views of the lake on your left-hand side.

❸ The path will drop down to be level with the lake at the optimistically named Boathouse Promenade. *The stone structure was built in the 1830s but although accommodating a boat at lake level, it was principally a sluice house controlling the outflow of water. This function ceased in 2012 when water management was dealt with by way of culverts allowing fish (there are plenty of carp in the lake) to access the River Len.* When you get to the far end of the lake, having passed the boathouse, keep left and follow the waterside path across the small bridge and up the gentle hill. The main park café is up a few steps on the right. Keep following the lake on your left-hand side. Where the main tarmac path bears right behind the café, take the unsurfaced path ahead. This path will soon rejoin another tarmac path which you now follow all the way around the side of the lake. Continue where it drops down and crosses the end of the lake over a bridge. Keep ahead in the same direction and shortly you will be back at point 2. You now retrace your steps back to the start.

Walk 16
PEGWELL BAY
3½ miles (5.6 km)

Start: Pegwell Road. **Sat Nav:** CT11 0NJ.

Parking: Although close to the clifftop, as there is no beach access from here, there is usually plenty of unrestricted on-street parking in Pegwell Road. We suggest driving down as far as the hotel to scout out any available spaces close to the pub and then driving back up again until you find a space.

Map: OS Explorer 150 Canterbury & Isle of Thanet.
Grid Ref: TR363641.

This is a coastal walk starting on top of the cliffs on one side of the bay and dropping down to a loop of a country park on the other. The name Pegwell Bay isn't usually associated with international travel, but there is a theme to this walk – of cross-channel traffic hundreds of years apart.

THE SIR STANLEY GRAY pub is at the start of the walk. What it may lack in its external appearance it more than makes up for with a stunning terrace overlooking the bay. Favoured by locals, on a sunny day and out of the wind it's a great spot for

> **Terrain:** The main walk is mostly flat with a long easy gradient from the clifftop down to the bay and back. Dedicated paths along the top of the cliffs and in the country park, with a short distance of roadside pavement walking.
>
> **Livestock & Stiles:** None encountered. No stiles.
>
> **Dog Friendly?** Yes.

sitting at the tables looking out to sea. Open from 11.30 daily. ☎ 01843 599590. **THE VIKING SHIP CAFE** is on the green at Cliffsend at point 2 of the walk.

The Walk

1 From outside the Sir Stanley Gray pub and facing the hotel across the road, turn left and a few metres later turn left again along the coast path. It starts off as a track and then, after the Coast Guard cottages on the right, it is a clifftop path. About ½ mile later, keep ahead across an access road. When you get to the next marker post, bear right following the yellow waymarker up towards the houses. Just before you get to the mini roundabout turn left down the tarmac path onto the green. The café is on the left.

2 *You can't fail to spot our first example of international travel in the form of the Viking ship, Hugin, which takes centre stage on the green.*

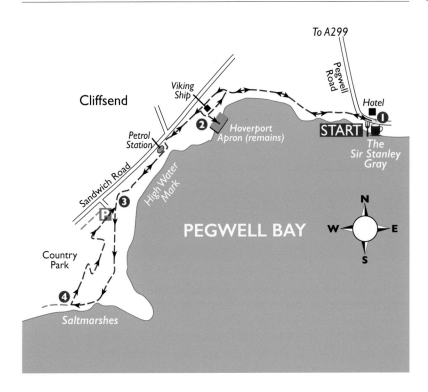

Although a replica, this very ship was sailed from Denmark in 1949 to mark the 1500th anniversary of the arrival in Kent of Viking brothers Hengist and Horsa, who, according to the legend, landed nearby in AD 449. Hengist later became the first Saxon king of Kent. Keep along the broad shared cycle path parallel to the road. For a short distance you will be walking along the pavement right next to the road until just before you reach a petrol station. Turn left following the signpost for cycle way 15 which goes behind the petrol station next to the salt marshes.

❸ When you get to the Country Park keep left along the raised embankment. Pass a car park on the right-hand side, then keep ahead with Pegwell Bay on your left. Pass the bird hide on your left. *The saltmarsh and mudflats at low tide provide a wealth of food for flocks of wading birds. The bay is an internationally important site for migrating and wintering wetland birds.* Keep to the path as it swings right following the line of the marshes.

Remains of the hoverport apron

4 At the end of the marshes follow the red Country Park arrow waymarker with the route now doglegging right. Follow this broad grassy path as it meanders back across the country park. In the 1960s this green was the local municipal refuse dump. After it closed as a waste site it was capped with soil and landscaped. Keep following the red arrows and the path will eventually bring you back past the children's playground, the car park and back to point 3. You now retrace your route back to point 2. *As you do so, you will see an enormous area of abandoned concrete jutting out to sea. This is all that remains of the International Ramsgate Hoverport terminal and maintenance base, opened in 1969. Run by the company Hoverlloyd, there were up to 27 daily departures to Calais. At its busiest, 1¼ million passengers set off from Pegwell Bay for France each year. The terminal closed to passengers in 1982 after the company merged with rival British Rail's hovercraft operation, which was centred in Dover. The site was abandoned as a maintenance base in 1987 and the buildings were demolished in the 1990s. Heavily overgrown and returning to nature, the concrete hovercraft pad, car-marshalling area and approach road are all that remain.* When you get back to the Viking ship you can turn right just before it and go down the steps to the remains of the hoverport concrete apron if you wish to get a closer look. Returning to the walk you can turn right after you have climbed back up the steps to return back to the route and retrace your steps to the start.

Walk 17
SANDWICH
3½ miles (5.6 km)

Start: Gazen Salts Car Park. **Sat Nav:** CT13 9EU.

Parking: Gazen Salts pay and display public car park.

Map: OS Explorer 150 Canterbury & Isle of Thanet.
Grid Ref: TR329585.

This is a walk around one of the most historic towns in Kent, with plenty to see and do, including strolling along the old town walls before heading off into the countryside and returning along a pleasant riverbank. One of the Cinque Ports, Sandwich claims to be one of the best-preserved medieval towns in England. Its most famous historical figure is John Montagu, 4th Earl of Sandwich, who supposedly invented the sandwich in 1762 at the gambling table, when he asked for meat to be served between slices of bread to avoid interrupting the game.

As a tourist centre, the town has a whole variety of pubs, cafés and restaurants. Near the end of the walk we'd recommend the **CRISPIN INN**, dating from 1491 and right next to the

Waterside Walks in Kent

> **Terrain:** Paved paths in town. Grassy and tarmac paths out of town. Flat and very easy.
>
> **Livestock & Stiles:** None encountered. No stiles.
>
> **Dog Friendly?** Yes.

Barbican gate. Log fires in winter and a patio close to the river for the summer. ☎ 01304 621967. If you are looking for a café, the **STRAND STREET KITCHEN**, also with some outside courtyard seating, is worth a stop for homemade cakes, 28 Strand Street. ☎ 01304 612525.

The Walk

1 Leave the car park at the pedestrian exit at the far end. At the playing fields bear right up the embankment with the river now on your right. Keep ahead as the path follows the loops in the river. At the end, where the path drops down onto a road, go through the gate and turn left along the pavement.

2 Just before you get to the fire station, take the path on the left across the small green. This is Gallows Field where hangings took place until the 18th century. Then cross the road and turn right down The Butts. *The Butts were used in medieval times as an archery practice field. Every male inhabitant over the age of 12*

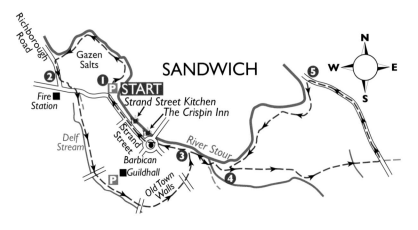

was expected to practise after church on Sunday in case of a raid by the French. In 1415 it is claimed Henry V's archers practised here before sailing to victory at Agincourt. You are now walking on top of what were the old town walls. You will soon have the Delf Stream watercourse and cricket ground on your right-hand side. *Dutch engineers (famous for creating polders in Holland) improved the Delf Stream to both irrigate adjacent fields and provide the town with a water supply that was still used until the late 1800s.* Keep ahead along the path and cross the next road. If you want to visit the old town, take the left-hand turn down the footpath marked Fellowship Walk and cut across the car park to the 16th-century Guildhall which contains a fascinating free museum including a 14th-century copy of the *Magna Carta*. Returning to the walk, cross the next road. Keep going along the raised town walls, crossing a couple of roads as you go. The straight and long section named Ropewalk was used for 'walking out' in the rope-making process. The town wall was built in 1385 by order of King Richard II.

3 When you finally come out at a children's playground, drop down a few steps, cross the playground and turn sharp right along the combined footpath and cycle way, now with the river on your left-hand side. Cross the first footbridge on the left. Ignore the first dead-end footpath on the right which only leads to a fenced-off sluice.

4 Keep ahead on the tarmac path. Where the path emerges onto a tarmac track, turn left.

5 Take the next footpath on the left behind some palisade fencing up onto the riverbank. With the river on your right, continue

along this path which will bring you back to point 3. Now keep to the riverside path with the river on your right-hand side. This will bring you out at the quayside. At the bridge at the far end, go through or around the Barbican Gate and then turn first right down Strand Street. *The Barbican dates from the late 14th century. What used to be the main road north passes between the towers. The small house next to it was occupied by the toll collector for the adjacent bridge over the Stour. The tradition of charging a fee to cross the river goes back to the 11th century when King Canute granted the monks of Canterbury a charter to charge for a ferry crossing in the days when the river was much wider.* Strand Street is said to contain more half-timbered houses than any other street in England. On the right the King's Lodging, which dates from 1400, takes its name from royal visitors Henry VIII and Elizabeth I. Continuing ahead, the car park will be on the right-hand side.

Walk 18
TONBRIDGE
5 miles (8 km)

Start: Haysden Country Park. **Sat Nav:** TN11 9BB.

Parking: At the country park pay & display car park.

Map: OS Explorer 147, Sevenoaks & Tonbridge.
Grid Ref: TQ570459.

This walk takes you around the watery environs of Tonbridge. As well as the River Medway, which flows through the middle of the town, there are streams, lakes, watercourses and old canals to explore. The walk takes in the town's formal park, an adjacent country park and an area of recent riverside urban regeneration, not to mention the remains of an imposing 13th-century castle.

> **Terrain:** Mostly flat, one easy gradient up into Powder Mills village. A few hundred metres along a quiet lane, short distances along access roads and a few metres along and crossing the town's High Street. Otherwise there are mainly good paths, some of which are tarmacked.
>
> **Livestock & Stiles:** None encountered, but be aware of waterfowl. No stiles.
>
> **Dog Friendly?** Yes.

There is a café at the car park with outdoor seating. Opening times vary. The usual variety of high street establishments is also on hand, near point 4 on the walk. **SIXTY FIVE MM COFFEE** offers what might be the best coffee in town and is situated right on the walk next to the High Street bridge opposite the castle. The **HUMPHREY BEAN**, a Wetherspoon conversion of an old post office with a large open air area at the back is a few doors down from the bridge, but does not allow dogs. There are plenty of benches at the refurbished Moorings for an impromptu picnic with provisions picked up in the town.

The Walk

1 Exit the car park passing the toilets and café on the right-hand side. Continue underneath the railway bridge. At Barden Lake bear right and do a circuit of the lake. Just before you are back at the benches bear right into the trees and then right across Sharpe's Bridge over the water channel. Once you've crossed the bridge turn left following the sign to the Leigh Barrier along the broad riverside path, keeping the river on your right-hand side. *Haysden Country Park is criss-crossed by a variety of watercourses, many of them man-made to try to make the River Medway more navigable to commercial shipping in the 19th century. The channel on the right, known as Long Reach was dug in 1829 to straighten a part of the river for this purpose. The Park is home to a rich variety of wildlife.*

2 Cross the river at the next bridge (Friendship Bridge) on the right-hand side. Then take the path straight ahead across the field into the trees. Follow the path through the trees to the top,

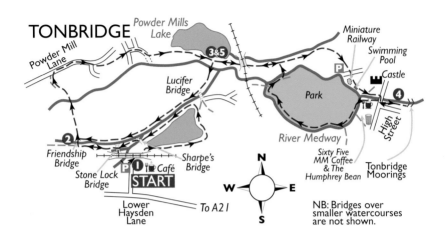

go through the gate and continue along the drive. At the end turn right into the lane. Where the lane bears left at the junction with Burton Avenue take the footpath straight ahead. With a housing development on the right, keep ahead, then cross the next residential road. At the end bear right down the small road named Hunter Seal and then a few metres later keep to the footpath on the left-hand side.

❸ Turn left immediately after the path bears away from the lake and crosses a small bridge, with the river now on your right-hand side. There will be a short divergence of paths a little later but it doesn't matter which one you take. Pass underneath the low railway bridge then go to the left-hand side of the hedgeline following the National Cycle Network 12 sign. Keep ahead along the tarmac path keeping the water channel on your left-hand side. Don't take the path into the park or the floodlit sportsground. At the far end cross the car park access road with the miniature railway on the right. Turn slightly left at the swimming pool, cross the river then bear right keeping the river on your right-hand side. The entrance to the castle grounds, which is free of charge, will soon be on your left. *You can still climb the 1000-year-old motte or castle mound where the first Norman castle would have stood at the top. The 13th-century gatehouse is said to be the best preserved example in England. The massive curtain walls date from the same time. In the 18th century,*

Tonbridge Castle

stone was taken from the walls to build the mansion next to the gatehouse, which now serves as the local tourist information centre. Continuing the walk, keep ahead to the High Street bridge. Cross the bridge and cross the road, take the first side road on the left and, then a few metres later, double back down to the river bank and turn right. Continue a short distance along the riverside path to Tonbridge Moorings.

4 Retrace your steps back to the bridge and re-cross the road. Now walk down the other side of the river, keeping it on your right-hand side. Cross the first bridge on the right-hand side and then immediately turn left down the footpath called Riverside Walk. Walk round the perimeter of the park, and take the 4th bridge across the river. This follows the main tarmac path (the 3rd bridge is quite hidden). Cross the river, follow the path to the far end, then turn left (you will now be briefly retracing your steps from the earlier route), returning back underneath the low railway bridge.

5 Turn left following the National Cycle Network 12 sign. Cross two small bridges in short succession and then continue ahead with the river on your left and the fields on your right. When you get to the next bridge on your left (Lucifer Bridge), keep ahead with the river still on your left-hand side. (If you want to cut the walk slightly short here, turn left over the bridge and follow the path, then keep right, through to Bardon Lake where you will join the first part of the walk.) To continue, carry on ahead keeping the river on your left-hand side all the way to Friendship Bridge (point 2 on the walk). Cross the bridge then turn left, retracing your steps back a short way along your earlier route. Now take the right-hand turn at Stone Lock Bridge. When you cross the bridge, if you look down, you can see how it got its name. *These are the remains of a lock built in 1829 that was the start of an attempt to build a canal to Penshurst. It is claimed that some of the massive hand-finished stone blocks were taken from Tonbridge Castle. Although a mile of the canal was dug, it never filled with water and the failed attempt saw the promoter fleeing to America to escape his debts.* Continue underneath the railway and then turn next left. Cross the bridge back to the car park and the start.

Walk 19
WAREHORNE & APPLEDORE
7½ miles (12 km)

Start: The Street, Appledore. **Sat Nav:** TN26 2AF.

Parking: Plenty of unrestricted parking in Appledore village, with a free car park also available.

Map: OS Explorer 125, Romney Marsh, Rye & Winchelsea.
Grid Ref: TQ956296.

This walk skirts the north-west edge of Romney Marsh and features the Royal Military Canal, built here as a defensive measure when the country was in fear of invasion from Napoleonic France. It takes in a couple of charming villages, ancient churches, some fine views and an excellent pub.

The 16th-century **WOOLPACK INN** at Warehorne (point 4 on the walk, opposite the village church) is just about everything you could want in a country pub. An ideal place to sit outside and watch the world go by. Local ales are from Pig & Porter (Tunbridge Wells) and Romney Marsh (New Romney). ☎ 01233 732900. **MISS MOLLETT'S HIGH CLASS TEA ROOM** (clearly not underselling themselves, but nonetheless recommended) is in Appledore village. Open 10-4, closed Mondays & Tuesdays. ☎ 01233 758555.

Waterside Walks in Kent

> **Terrain:** Mostly footpaths or very quiet country lanes. Pavement walking in Appledore village and a very short stretch along a busier road where care needs to be taken. A few longish gradients, but they are gentle.
>
> **Livestock & Stiles:** Cattle in the field approaching Warehorne. Sheep – everywhere! No stiles.
>
> **Dog Friendly?** Yes, however whilst we have avoided paths with stiles in order to make the walk dog friendly, this is part of Romney Marsh, which is world renowned for its population of sheep. You will find sheep grazing around all the footpaths on this walk, and consequently it will mean dogs need to be on leads.

The Walk

1 Follow Appledore's broad main street, The Street, all the way down, past the church on the left-hand side, to the Royal Military Canal. When you get to the canal take the footpath on the left-hand side just before the bridge. *After Napoleon had invaded parts of Europe in the late 18th century, Britain feared she would be next. The canal was built as a water obstacle to halt the advance of this possible French invasion. Building started in 1804 and took so long it was only finished after any realistic threat of invasion had receded.* Continue with the canal on your right-hand side. You have the choice (most of the way) of walking on top of the earth bank or the broader track, the former military road, at the lower level.

2 When you get to the first road turn left up the lane. Ignore the first footpath on the right. Carry on walking up the lane, turn right into Church Road, and then, when you get to the top, take the first footpath on the right. Follow the footpath around the left-hand field boundary and through the gate into the churchyard on the left-hand side. The churchyard gate is the second gate on the left and is slightly obscured by trees. The first gate leads into a private garden.

3 Turn right, keeping the church on your left. *It is claimed that the site of the church was once the scene of a battle, being stormed by the Danes in the 10th century. The tower is nearly 900 years old, with most of the rest of the church dating from the 13th century. The*

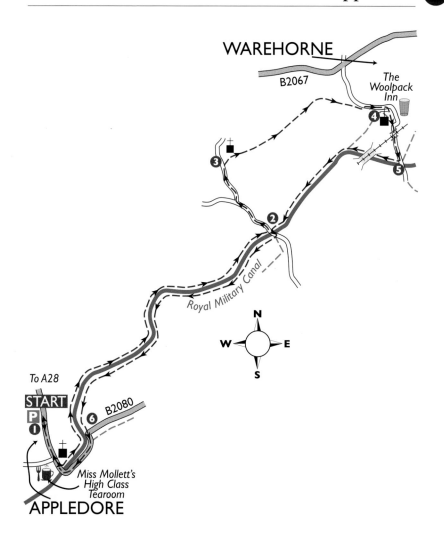

church was originally larger, but was reduced in size after being struck by lightning in 1559. Until 2013 there was no mains electricity and winter church services were still held using candlelight. Leave the churchyard through the gate at the far end. You will now see the church tower of Warehorne, the next village, on the horizon ahead of you, which is the direction you are heading in. At the bottom of the field go through the gate bearing slightly right and then follow the right-hand fenceline. Cross three small bridges

over watercourses, and then cross two fields heading in the same direction. At the treeline at the top go through the gate bearing slightly right following the waymarker. Follow the path across the next large field and at the far end, at the top, go through the gate straight ahead. The path through the next smaller field is a little indistinct but you will now see the church tower ahead of you. Keep in that direction. Go through the gate at the end, turn left a few metres down the access road and then turn right into the lane. *The first recorded mention of Warehorne is in an Anglo-Saxon charter of Ecgberht, King of Wessex (AD 770-839), where it is called Werehornas. The* Domesday Book *mentions the village and states that there was a church here, but the earliest part of the existing building dates from 1200.* The Woolpack Inn will shortly be on your left-hand side.

4 Opposite the pub take the short path up to the church, don't cross the first stile on the right-hand side but take the footpath that hugs the church right up against its right-hand wall. *Take in the view. Around 6000BC, Romney Marsh did not exist. From here it is easy to appreciate that the great flat expanse of the marshes*

ahead and to the left of you were once beneath the sea and you are standing on what would have been the original coastline of a great bay. It's likely that what is now the gently sloping churchyard may even have been a cliff top, steadily eroded over millennia. Go through the little gate next to the church wall and then downhill through the churchyard. Go through the gate at the end, and then bear right down the lane and over the level crossing.

5 When you get back to the canal take the footpath on the right-hand side just before the bridge. Passing the pillbox on the left, carry on underneath the railway bridge. *In 1940, Nazi Germany's invasion plan included crossing the flat Romney Marsh. The canal resumed a defensive role and was re-equipped with troops, concrete pillboxes, and metal obstacles. It is unlikely the canal would have been much of an impediment to a 20th-century mechanised war machine, but the idea was to buy time.* Keep ahead with the canal on your left-hand side. Again you can take the higher path on top of the bank or the broader path lower down. After a while you'll get some good views back over the fields to Kenardington church. When you get to the lane at point 2, turn left, cross the bridge, and then immediately turn right. Go through the permissive car park and carry on walking ahead, now with the canal on your right-hand side.

6 When you get to the road, go through the gate and turn right. Follow this road back across the bridge over the canal and retrace your way back up into Appledore village. The tea room will be on your left.

Walk 20
WATERINGBURY & TESTON LOCK
4 miles (6.4 km)

Start: Bow Road, Wateringbury. **Sat Nav:** ME18 5EB.

Parking: Plenty of unrestricted parking in the side roads off Bow Road.

Map: OS Explorer 148, Maidstone & The Medway Towns.
Grid Ref: TQ690528.

An idyllic walk along an iconic part of the River Medway as it twists and turns through the valley. Distinctive oast houses with their white cowls dot the landscape – this part of Kent was one of the centres of the hop-growing industry. From the village of Wateringbury you walk along the Medway Valley Path, taking in views of the valley as far as medieval Teston Bridge with its country park and lock, before heading back along the popular riverside path.

> **Terrain:** One short but steepish climb, otherwise flat and easy. The route is along popular, mostly well-marked paths. A short section along a quiet lane and about 100 metres on a more busy road.
>
> **Livestock & Stiles:** Horses in the fields around points 1 and 2. At Teston there are usually signs when cattle are grazing in the meadow near the lock. No stiles.
>
> **Dog Friendly?** Yes, no obstructions. However, be aware that animals may be in some fields and in places there are signs from landowners requesting dogs be kept on leads.

THE RAILWAY at Wateringbury is right at the start of the walk. Sometimes not open until mid-afternoon. ☎ 01622 812911. There is a small café fronting the river in Bow Bridge Marina, also at the beginning of the walk. It's not unusual to find an ice cream van in the car park at Teston.

The Walk

❶ Walk down to the railway station from wherever you have parked. Cross over the level crossing and over the bridge across the River Medway. The marina café is through the yard on the right. Once you have crossed the bridge take the footpath on the left. Go through the gate into the field. Don't be misled by the waymarker suggesting you should be on the left-hand side of the fenceline; that path goes nowhere. Once you are in the field take the immediate left fork of paths. Keep ahead in the same direction. In the early summer you will be walking through flower-strewn meadows. When the path emerges from a wood the direction to go is a little unclear – you need to bear right up the side of the hill. You will soon have great views looking down back across the river.

❷ Once over the brow of the hill, continue ahead through the gate and onto the tarmac drive, and on through the refurbished farmyard. Just before you get to the oast houses and the barn, at the very top, there is a gate and stile on the left-hand side, go through this. *The distinctive oast houses in the landscape here are designed for drying*

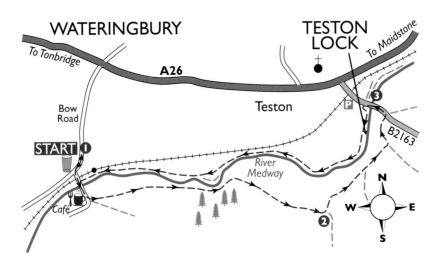

hops as part of the brewing process. *They usually consist of a rectangular building and one or more kilns (usually, but not always circular) in which the hops were spread out to be dried by hot air rising from a wood or charcoal fire below. The drying floors were perforated to permit the heat to pass through and escape through a cowl in the roof which turned with the wind. Many in Kent have been converted for residential use.* The public footpath is not very clear at this point but there is a signpost in the middle of the field ahead of you which points the way. The driveway here soon becomes a public right of way with great views down on the left towards Teston Lock. You will also pass a Second World War pillbox on the left-hand side. Keep ahead through the gate in between the houses. Continue along the lane in the same direction as it bears left and drops downhill. At the end, when you emerge onto a busier road, turn left and shortly you'll be crossing the medieval six-arch Teston Bridge. *Dating back to the 14th century and made with Kentish ragstone, the bridge is a well-known feature in the area. The central arch was rebuilt at the end of the 18th century to improve navigation on the river. Three other arches were rebuilt in 1830, and the whole bridge was restored in 1978.* Take extra care when crossing.

3 Immediately you have crossed the bridge, take the footpath on the left and walk down to the river, and then turn right away from the bridge. *This is Teston Bridge Country Park, which comprises three*

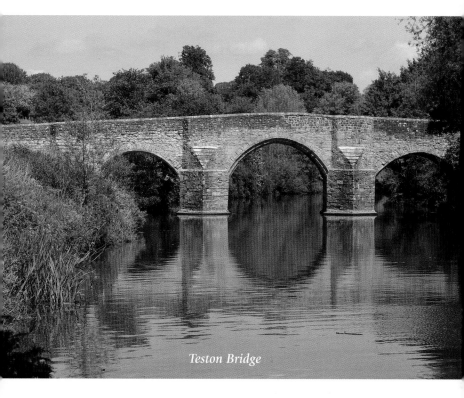

Teston Bridge

meadows, riverside walks and the lock. It was converted from grazing land to an open public space in 1978. Now keep going along the riverside path with the river on your left. Bear left at the fork in the path, this will take you along the edge of Teston Lock itself. *There has been a lock and weir at Teston since the 1740s. It was one of 14 built to make the Medway navigable and allow commercial boats to bring cargo to and from the middle of the county at Tonbridge. The level of the river drops two metres as it heads downstream. Look out for the ghostly ivy covered ruins of the linseed oil and cattle cake mill on the other side of the river. Built in 1809, reputedly by famous architect John Rennie, it burned down in 1885. The current lock dates from 1911.* You now carry on ahead in the same direction, keeping to the riverside path all the way back to Wateringbury and the start of the walk. At a few points there are 'Private' signs, but these refer to mooring rights, not your right to be on the public footpath. Eventually the path will return you back to the starting point.

OTHER TITLES FROM COUNTRYSIDE BOOKS

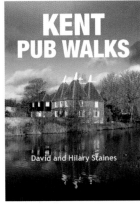
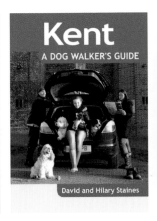

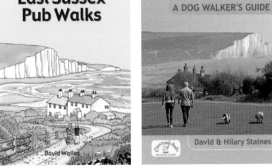

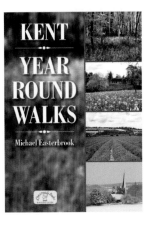

To see our full range of books please visit
www.countrysidebooks.co.uk
Follow us on @CountrysideBooks